INSIGHT COMPACT GUIDES

SING

Compact Guide: Singapore is the ideal quick-reference guide to the Asian city-state. It tells you all you need to know about Singapore's attractions, from Raffles Hotel to Orchard Road, Chinatown to Little India, and Arab Street to Sentosa Island, taking in the city's parks, gardens and other recreation spots on the way, as well as providing detailed information on where to shop and dine.

This is just one title in *Apa Publications'* new series of pocket-sized, easy-to-use guidebooks intended for the independent-minded traveller. *Compact Guides* pride themselves on being up-to-date and authoritative. They are in essence mini travel encyclopedias, designed to be comprehensive yet portable, as well as readable and reliable.

Star Attractions

An instant reference to some of Singapore's most popular tourist attractions to help you on your way.

Raffles Hotel p26

Orchard Road p27–31

Chinatown p32–7

Thian Hock Keng Temple p34

Little India p38–41

Arab Street p42–3

Sentosa Island p44–7

Geylang Serai Market p51

Merlion p23

Mandai Orchid Garden p58

Harbour boats p58–9

Singapore

Introduction

Singapore – Southeast Asia City State..5
Historical Highlights 16

Places

Route 1: The Colonial District **20**
Route 2: Orchard Road **27**
Route 3: Chinatown..**32**
Route 4: Little India..**38**
Route 5: Arab Street **42**
Route 6: Sentosa...**44**
Route 7: Jurong..**48**
Route 8: The Malay and Peranakan Quarters...........................**50**
Route 9: The Other Islands..**53**
Further Sights..**55**
Excursions:
       Johor Bahru **60**
       Kukup..**60**
       Desaru **60**
       Melaka..**61**
       Batam Island..**61**

Culture

Art and Customs **63**
Festivals **67**

Leisure

Food and Drink **71**
Shopping and Markets **79**
Nightlife **82**

Practical Information

Getting There **85**
Getting Around **86**
Facts for the Visitor..**89**
Accommodation..**93**

Index **96**

Singapore – Southeast Asia's City State

Singapore's name derives from an optical illusion. According to legend, at some time in the 14th century, when the island was part of the huge Sri Vijaya empire, a visiting prince from Sumatra thought he saw a lion – in the middle of a tropical rain forest where the predator, normally at home on open plains, would never go. The prince was so certain he had seen a lion that he called the island at the southern tip of Malaysia 'Singa Pura' or 'Lion City'. The merlion, a mythical creature with a lion's head and a fish's tail, later became the state symbol of Singapore.

Merlion – symbol of Singapore

The island slumbered on until the 19th century when an Englishman named Stamford Raffles identified the settlement, with its naturally sheltered harbour, as being of great strategic maritime importance. On 6 February 1819 he purchased the land from the then ruler, the Sultan of Johor, and obtained permission to establish a trading post for the British East India Company. At last the English had gained a foothold in this part of the world which until then had been firmly under Dutch control. As a free port, Singapore attracted commercial vessels from all over the world. More and more Europeans, particularly the English, saw good business prospects here and settled on the tropical island in large numbers. Cheap labour was urgently required and so hard-working Chinese and Indians, eager to escape the poverty and hunger of their homeland, were recruited.

5

By the middle of the 19th century, Europe and Asia had been brought closer together by the advent of steamships, the telegraph and also the opening of the Suez Canal. Even the doubters had to admit it: the British had got a bargain, quite apart from the strategic importance of gaining a military presence in the Far East. Because of its strong defensive installations, Singapore was regarded as virtually impregnable – until 1942, that is, when it took Japanese troops only a few weeks to capture the British base. Using the road and rail causeway from Malaysia to Singapore, the unstoppable enemy soldiers arrived on, of all things, bicycles.

Since then, something remarkable has happened in Singapore. No new arrival at the city's ultra-modern airport today can fail to be impressed: polished marble, fountains, orchids, soft upholstery, tidy rows of shops and spotlessly clean toilets. The slums, epidemics, poverty, crime and poor hygiene that some first-time visitors still expect to find in Southeast Asia have been eradicated. The food is safe to eat, even from the street stalls, and the streets are virtually crime-free. Visitors now marvel at the orderliness, the new residential districts, the skyscrapers and the restored streets.

Singapore today

Situation and landscape

The island state of Singapore lies about 137km (85 miles) north of the equator, just off the southern tip of Malaysia. It is linked to the mainland by a 1.1-km long embankment, known as the Causeway. About 60 small islands also belong to Singapore, the largest being Tekong, Ubin and Sentosa. The main island measures 23km (14 miles) from north to south and 42km (26 miles) from east to west. The landscape is gently undulating, with large parts no more than 15m (50ft) above sea level. At 165m (541ft), Bukit Timah stands at the centre of the island. Granite and other hard rocks determined the original landscape. Steep inclines of sedimentary rock dominate the west and southwest, e.g. Mount Faber. Apart from a few cliffs, the coast line is generally flat, although in a number of places its course has been changed considerably by man. Harbours have been created, mangrove swamps drained and the natural contours altered by bulldozers. There are only a few small watercourses, but many man-made canals to drain off the heavy tropical rainfall. The longest river, the Sungei Seletar is 15km (9 miles) long.

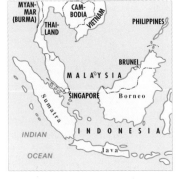

Climate and when to go

The tropical climate of Singapore is hot and humid with the average temperature hovering around 27°C (80°F). During the daytime, it often goes above 30°C (86°F), but there are no great fluctuations. Humidity is high, and varies between 64 and 96 percent. The northeast monsoon blows from December to March, and the southwest from June to September, but the wind speeds are light, all year round. Spectacular thunderstorms occur frequently between the monsoons, in April–May and October–November. Most offices, shopping centres, underground train stations and homes are air-conditioned and this makes it easier for Singaporeans to cope with the sweltering temperatures.

Flora and fauna

Exploring Bukit Timah

It is hard to believe, but the island of Singapore was once tropical jungle. When Stamford Raffles and his crew dropped anchor off the coast in the early 19th century, they found impenetrable mangrove forests lining the shore. Natural vegetation now only occurs in conservation areas such as the Bukit Timah Nature Reserve. Hard wood trees up to 40m (130ft) tall remain in the surviving primeval forest, but the mangroves have largely disappeared.

Despite all the building work, Singapore is not about to become a concrete desert. As well as the nature reserves, there are numerous parks and gardens, and the huge Botanical Garden amid the sea of houses has a large collection

Botanical Gardens

7

of plants and trees. Nevertheless, about 80 percent of the species growing here are not native. The lush bougainvillea which adorn the cityscape originated in South America, the rubber tree comes from Brazil.

Singapore is famous for its rare and colourful orchids, many of which are cultivated and then exported. Packaged flowers can be bought at the airport and taken home as presents or souvenirs. Lovers of flowers will certainly want to visit the breathtakingly beautiful Mandai Orchid Gardens *(see page 58)*.

It is often difficult to identify certain orchids as there are so many different shapes and colours. Some have brightly-coloured, fleshy petals, others flower modestly in the background. Many of them embed their roots very firmly in the bark of a tree. One typical feature of orchids is the 'labellum', the most striking and most unusual of the six petals. 'Vanda Miss Joaquim', the national orchid of Singapore, has a deep violet labellum. When a new hybrid is developed, the Singaporean botanists often have difficulty knowing what to call it and famous visitors to the city often discover that a new orchid has been christened after them.

One of many species at the Mandai Orchid Gardens

Most of the native fauna live in the natural woodland. Lemurs and squirrels are plentiful, as are lizards, snakes, frogs and bats, but Singapore is particularly proud of its birdlife. Over 320 different species have been recorded, most of them migratory birds from the northern hemisphere, which overwinter near the equator.

While lions have never lived on the island, tigers certainly have, but they were mercilessly hunted to extinction during the 19th century. The last freely roaming tiger was shot in the Raffles Hotel billiard room in 1902; it had escaped from a travelling circus. When Singapore zoo *(see page 57)* was opened in 1974, tigers were re-introduced, but they are locked away inside a secure enclosure.

Resident at Jurong Bird Park

A new generation of Moslems

Population

Singapore has made remarkably rapid economic strides and has become a wealthy and independent state. The efficient infrastructure has proved extremely attractive to multinationals and the city is often held up as a model for other countries of Southeast Asia. In fact, some of the city state's social policies are arousing a lot of interest among European and American politicians. This considerable feat owes much to the country's political structure, which actually bears little resemblance to western concepts of democracy and consensus. Before condemning the dominance of the government, however, outsiders should try to see Singapore in the context of the culture and attitudes of the various Asian races that live here.

'Many races, one nation, one Singapore' – this was the slogan used in the celebrations that marked the republic's 25th birthday in 1990 and it embodies the wish of the island's different races to work together for the prosperity of the nation – no easy task for 2.9 million people inhabiting a tiny island, particularly when the cultural heritage is so diverse. The overwhelming majority are Chinese (78 percent), the remainder are Malays (14 percent), Indians (7 percent) and other ethnic groups, such as Eurasians (1 percent).

Only the Malays can describe themselves as natives, as for hundreds of years their ancestors plied between the Malaysian mainland and the island. When in 1819 Stamford Raffles made his first trip up the Singapore River, all he discovered was a small Malay village with about 150 inhabitants, but that was soon to change. It was beside the mouth of the river where the first settlement was established. Immigrants flocked here in response to invitations from the prospering trading post and many came in the hope of finding work and a decent livelihood. The Malays were the first to arrive, followed by migrants from the Dutch-controlled Malacca region. Balinese, Javanese, Bugis (from the island of Celebes, now Sulawesi) also came in large numbers. Common cultural and religious strands between the islanders and the Malays quickly united these settlers.

The new arrivals from China, however, did not form such a homogeneous group. The first junk with Chinese immigrants arrived in February 1821. Although most came from the southern provinces of mainland China, they were known as Hokkiens, Teochews and Cantonese or Hakkas, depending on their native region and the dialect they spoke. The Hokkiens are still by far the largest dialect group. All of them wished to retain their cultural identity, whether by continuing to follow their traditional professions and religious rituals or by preparing their food according to their ancient customs. Initially, it was only the menfolk who ventured abroad and, of course, many of them then married Malay women.

The children from these relationships were called *Peranakans* or Straits Chinese, since their mothers originated from the Straits Settlements, as Malacca, Penang and Singapore were known. They were the first Asians to speak English and to adopt western customs. Their staunch loyalty to the colony led some to describe them cynically as the 'King's Chinese'. Inevitably, the *nonyas* (women) and *babas* (men) created a double culture. 'Inside Chinese, outside Malay' is one description that has been applied to the Peranakans, although they no longer exist as a distinct sector of the population. The often wealthy Peranakan families in Singapore, e.g. on Emerald Hill *(see Route 2, page 29)*, often left behind homes whose distinctive architectural style was just as typically Chinese as the coloured tiles on the facade.

The Chinese make up the majority

Around the middle of the 19th century, many Chinese women emigrated to Singapore with the encouragement of the British colonial authorities. By 1867 some 67 percent of the island's inhabitants were Chinese. In order to keep arguments and interracial conflict to a minimum, from the very beginning Raffles segregated the various ethnic groups. In Chinatown, the different dialect groups were allocated certain streets. Although the Chinese can speak Cantonese, Teochew etc, the Singapore authorities regard Mandarin as the official language of the Chinese community. English is the language of business and administration, but Malay and Tamil are also classified as official languages.

Little India *(see pages 38–41)* is the name given to the quarter initially settled by Indians. The first Indian settlers were immigrants, either from the southern part of India or

Residents of Little India

Sri Lanka. Several hundred of them were transported here by the British in 1823 and were housed in camps while working on roads and other buildings, such as St Andrew's Cathedral *(see page 23)*. Since 1950 it has been necessary to introduce tighter immigration laws to stem the tide of migrants from the sub-continent.

That the various ethnic groups and cultures have been able to work together is partly the result of the government's authoritarian leadership style. Since independence in 1965, the government has often relied on broad public education campaigns to put across its goals and aspirations to the man (and woman) in the street. Campaigns on the subjects of spitting, littering, flushing of public toilets, courtesy, water conservation, keeping fit, speaking of Mandarin instead of dialects amongst the Chinese, and even chewing gum, have sought to create national solidarity and an ordered and well-behaved population. One of the more controversial public campaigns was in 1987, when the Ministry of Health urged graduate mothers to have more children so that Singapore would have a bigger pool of intelligentsia in the next century.

But Singaporeans rarely respond angrily to the government's constant urgings towards self-improvement. Basically, everyone goes along with what those in power ordain – and they will probably continue to do so, as long as their material welfare remains secure. Striving for material gain and success is deeply ingrained in the Chinese psyche, although recently this approach has lost favour with the government. Shortly before his resignation, the long-serving prime minister Lee Kuan Yew condemned 'materialism without morals'. He invoked the basic values of Confucianism, namely that the individual is subordinate to the needs of the wider community. Prosperity, therefore, is not equated with the selfish free-for-all that is often the consequence of pure capitalism.

The happy couple

Nearly half of all women work and make a considerable contribution to the family income. Although significant numbers of women occupy key positions in the private and public sectors, most of the top and best paying positions are filled by men. Compared with other Asian countries, the Singaporean standard of living is relatively high. The average monthly income is S$2,000, a healthy figure by any standards. But given rising costs of living, including astronomical prices for cars and private houses, it is a sum that does not go very far in Singapore.

Housing

Despite the construction of huge apartment blocks in the suburbs, living space is still in short supply, so, often, young people are obliged to live with their parents. Only married couples and singles over the age of 35 are granted flats by the Housing Development Board (HDB). Home for almost 90 percent of Singaporeans is a flat in a multistorey block. The state has introduced a form of compulsory saving towards home ownership: a part of a worker's wages is set aside, not just as a nest egg for retirement but also for the purchase of a home. A new three-bedroom HDB flat in the suburbs, leased for 99 years, costs between S$200,000 and 250,000. The door behind the surrounding balcony will probably reveal the race of the owner. The Chinese often have a red pelmet stretched out above the door as a good luck symbol, Indians place a few lemon leaves behind the door frame, while the Malays invariably leave their prayer mat hanging to air over the railings.

Private apartments

11

Religion

Religious freedom exists in Singapore. Most Chinese are Buddhists, Confucians or Taoists or else they take a little from all three. Chinese temples are dedicated to a hotchpotch of saints who are worshipped when required. *Nirvana*, a state of blessedness in which all human desire is extinguished, is the ultimate goal for Buddhists. To reach this exalted state and achieve release from the cycle of birth and rebirth, it is necessary to lead a life full of good deeds. Everyone's fate rests in their own hands, as the quality of the next life depends on how the individual has behaved in his life.

Worship at the temple

Confucianism is derived from the teachings of Buddha, but more weight is placed on adherence to a set of moral values, which require the individual to bow to the wishes of the community. Taoism is also linked with Buddhism, but here, man is subjected to the will of nature. Life should follow its 'natural' course, in harmony and moderation and with modesty and meditation.

Most Malays are Moslems. Islam was brought to Malaysia in the 12th century by merchants from India and

Sultan Mosque and Hindu deity at the Sri Mariamman Temple

Arabia. According to the teachings of the prophet Mohammed, there is only one God, Allah. Every practising Moslem should pray to Allah five times each day, observe the annual fasting month of Ramadan and make a pilgrimage to Mecca at least once during his lifetime. Although the religious life of the Moslem community takes place away from the public gaze, the impact of Islam in Singapore is still considerable.

Most Indians are Hindus. The numerous Hindu gods are all manifestations of one god, the spirit Brahman, to whom everyone's being is subordinate. Like Buddhists, Hindus believe in rebirth. There are a number of ways to escape from this cycle: one way is through a life of asceticism and meditation; another way lies through good deeds, pilgrimages and an exemplary way of life. The caste system, an important element in Hindu society elsewhere, is not adhered to in modern Singapore.

Constitution and politics

When Singapore gained independence in 1959, the new state adopted a British-style parliamentary system. The president is the republic's head of state and he or she is elected by the people for a period of six years. In consultation with the party that commands a parliamentary majority, the president will appoint the prime minister and also the cabinet. The single-chamber parliament, the National Assembly, consists of 81 MPs and they are elected every five years. All Singaporeans aged 21 or over are entitled to vote.

The PAP (People's Action Party) has always been the majority party in parliament. Opposition parties such as the SDP (Singapore Democratic Party) and the WP (Workers' Party) have gradually increased their share of the popular vote, but, as minority parties, they have no real power.

Lee Kuan Yew was Singapore's prime minister for 31 years and was responsible for the city state's post-independence history. After four years in office, he notched up his first political victory. In 1963 Malaya and Singapore combined to form the Malaysian Federation. What worried the British most was the fear that the abandoned trading post was not going to be able to survive without a hinterland, so union with Malaya was seen as a sensible solution. But racial conflict and brawls between the dominant Chinese and the oppressed Malays destroyed the dream of a combined Southeast Asian nation. In 1965 Singapore left the Federation and established itself as an independent republic.

Singapore united

Since 1990 the government has been led by prime minister Goh Chok Tong, aided by a team of second generation leaders. As Senior Minister in the cabinet, Lee Kuan Yew, had smoothly guided the transition of leadership from the old guard, who achieved independence, to the new generation. Still, it is no secret that Lee continues to have a say in the running of the party. Maintaining internal security and social and political stability are still important aims, but some western critics believe that too much emphasis is placed on these policies.

13

Officially there is press freedom, but local publications are not known for departing conspicuously from the government line. The same is true of foreign newspapers and magazines, whose criticisms are condemned as an uninformed and unwarranted interference in Singapore's internal affairs. In 1994, for example, the government took libel action against the *International Herald Tribune*, after an article spoke of 'the compliant justice system of some Asian countries'. The writer, an American professor at a Singapore university, left for the US before court proceedings could take place.

And yet it would be wrong to describe Singapore as a completely authoritarian state. Singapore is a democracy, but one in which the underlying political and social assumptions have not been seriously questioned by a significant number of people. Censors ensure no pornographic material reaches the island. Prostitution is not forbidden, but it is not officially recognised. After a further tightening up of the drugs law, 'incurable addicts' face canings and imprisonment. Drug dealers, like murderers, can expect a death sentence if convicted.

Local laws
Practically every souvenir shop in Singapore sells white T-shirts printed with the warning of a fine for not flushing the toilet. Such fines are a serious matter for Singaporeans. Although in practice no one has ever been fined for not flushing toilets, the threat of a hefty fine is often

More symbols of the city

Freighters at the container port

deterrence enough. The police are conspicuous, and it's no accident that Singapore ranks as one of the world's safest countries. However, one does not have to be a hardened criminal to fall foul of the law. Improper behaviour, such as dropping litter, is enough, and spitting out a chewed-up wad of gum on the pavement can result in a S$500 fine. To reinforce this law, the import and export of chewing gum is forbidden, although Singaporeans can bring in a small amount for personal consumption. The laws about smoking in public places are likewise very strict.

Economy

The city state of Singapore has one of the highest living standards in Asia, indeed it is among the 20 wealthiest countries in the world. In 1996 Singapore lost its status within the OECD as a 'developing nation'. During the 1980s economic growth was always above 10 percent per annum. Although this rate slowed during the recession of the early 1990s, since 1994 it has been gradually rising again. In business circles, South Korea, Taiwan, Hong kong and Singapore are described as the 'Four Small Tigers'. 'Be the best that we can be' is a frequent battle cry and just one of the slogans that the government uses in its campaigns to spur on the people.

With no hinterland, no raw materials, no agricultural land, not even enough water to satisfy its own requirements (a pipeline from Malaysia keeps the taps running), the Singapore government had to come up with something special to provide a decent living for its people. One of the most important early decisions was to expand the port facilities and the harbour is now one of the biggest and busiest in the world. Round the clock, freighters are loaded and unloaded in the ultra-modern, electronically-controlled container port. Tankers from Brunei, Malaysia, In-

Bustling Clarke Quay

donesia and the Middle East supply oil to the massive refinery. Singapore's shipyards are among the most up-to-date in the world and cruise ships moor at a specially-built terminal. Situated at the hub of international air travel network, Singapore's Changi airport is another showpiece. New passenger records are broken every year and Singapore Airlines has earned a reputation as one of the world's most modern airlines. In 1995 Singapore welcomed 7 million tourists.

Immediately after the republic was founded, the government put the economy on an upward trend, as industry was transformed. Out went labour-intensive, low-profit trades such as textiles, in came companies specialising in high-value-added technologies such as communications and electronics. Incentives were given to foreign investors, as the government soon recognised the advantages of international capital. Only China has attracted more foreign investment in recent years. Many multinational companies have offices in the city and the foreign exchange market is of vital importance to the region. The turnover of the 90 or so banks that deal in foreign currencies exceeds that of their rivals in Hong Kong. For them the worldwide communication system has worked perfectly and Singaporean traders have a reputation for integrity in financial dealing – hence their embarrassment when the activities of Nick Leeson, the English trader, brought down Barings. Another factor has been Singapore's successful quest for new trading partners. The city state has benefited from its membership of the ASEAN (Association of Southeast Asian Nations). With so much economic activity, it is no surprise to learn that unemployment levels are currently around 2.7 percent.

Cottage industries

With rapid modernisation, the city's traditional crafts are hanging on grimly. The cottage industries that make masks for Chinese festivals, flower garlands for Indian temple visitors and incense for Buddhists are usually run from tiny, ground floor rooms in the older sections of Singapore. Basket-makers remain in Arab Street, goldsmiths in Little India and noodle makers in Chinatown, and their produce is often sold at the door near the 'five foot way', the local term for the five-foot wide pavement. These trades are slowly but surely dying out. For one thing, the skilled craftsmen can scarcely afford the ever-increasing rents in houses that are gradually undergoing restoration. The next generation is also unwilling to take over these trades, where skills have traditionally been handed down from father to son. Ambitious young Singaporeans see no future in eking out a meagre existence seven days a week from a tiny workshop.

Financial District

15

Flower garlands

Historical Highlights

Historians cannot agree on the first mention of Singapore, but it is said that the Chinese gave the name Pa-luo-chung to the island in the 3rd century AD. In 1330 a small settlement was discovered by a Chinese explorer and named Pancur. Singapore, often called Temasek in the literature of that period, was probably founded around the middle of the 13th century by the Javanese Sri Vijayan.

14–18th century First Siam (now Thailand), then Java (the Majapahit empire) seize the small island but show little interest in it. At the beginning of the 16th century, the Portuguese capture Malacca, then an important centre in east-west trade. In the 17th century, the island of Singapore is settled by about 100 Orang Lauts or sea nomads. At the end of the 18th century, the British and the 'British East India Company' open a trading post in Penang and take Malacca from the Dutch, who dominate the region at the time.

1819 On 29 January, Stamford Raffles (Governor of Bencoolen, West Sumatra) arrives in Singapore and the next day, with the help of the Sultan of Johor Riau (the southernmost province of Malaya) and the Temenggong, his representative on the island, opens a trading post for the East India Comany to deal with maritime traffic between China and India.

1824 The British agree to withdraw from Indonesia, in return for which the Dutch recognise British rights over Singapore. The Sultan cedes Singapore in perpetuity to the British.

1826 The trading stations at Penang, Malacca and Singapore are named the 'Straits Settlements', under the control of British India.

1867 On 1 April Singapore becomes a British Crown Colony, controlled by the Colonial Office in London. The population stands at 80,000, most of them Chinese.

End of the 19th century The Suez Canal opens and the number of ships calling in at Singapore increases. Trade flourishes. John Ridley, director of the Botanical Gardens in Singapore, succeeds in growing a rubber tree. The Malaysian peninsula and Singapore develop into the world's main rubber producers. In 1888 John Dunlop invents the rubber tyre.

1923 Singapore is linked to Malaysia by a causeway.

1942 The Japanese, led by General Tomoyuki Yamashita, invade and occupy Singapore.

1945–48 The Allies defeat the Japanese in the Far East. Singapore reverts to Crown Colony status.

1955 The Rendel Constitution granted by the British leads to elections and David Marshall becomes chief minister. A legislative council consisting of 32 members, 25 of whom are elected, is established. The Labour Front have a majority, but the PAP (People's Action Party) forms a powerful opposition.

1956 After failing to negotiate complete independence from the Crown, Marshall resigns and is replaced as chief minister by Lim Yew Hock.

1958 A constitutional agreement for partial independence for Singapore is finally signed in London, providing for a fully-elected legislative assembly, which, however, would have no power over external affairs and no absolute control of an internal security council.

1959 The first general election for the fully legislative assembly results in Lee Kuan Yew becoming prime minister as leader of the victorious PAP, which wins an absolute majority (43 out 51 seats – with 53 percent of the popular vote).

1963 The people of Malaya, Sarawak, North Borneo (now Sabah) and Singapore vote to form the Federation of Malaysia.

1965 Singapore leaves the Federation of Malaysia and becomes an independent sovereign nation, a member of both the United Nations and the Commonwealth.

1967 Singapore, Malaysia, Thailand, Indonesia, the Philippines and Brunei form a political and economic union known as the ASEAN (Association of Southeast Asian Nations).

1968 In the general election the PAP win all 58 seats.

1970–89 The PAP continues to dominate parliament, but at the start of the 1980s, Lee Kuan Yew's party has to live with an opposition party.

1981 In a by-election, Mr J.B. Jeyaratnam of the Workers' Party wins the first seat to be held by an opposition member.

1990 Lee Kuan Yew retires as prime minister and is replaced by Goh Chok Tong.

1996 As a result of a decision by the OECD, Singapore is no longer regarded as a 'developing nation'.

Who was Sir Stamford Raffles?

Thomas Stamford Bingley Raffles was born at sea off the coast of Jamaica on 6 July 1781. At the age of 15, he found work as an official with the East India Company. This expanding company was always on the look-out for new trading outlets and Raffles was driven partly by wanderlust and partly by ambition to explore the coast of Southeast Asia. In Java he discovered the temple city of Borobudur (for which he was knighted).

He was not favoured by the ruling Conservatives but that did not prevent him from winning an important place in the pantheon of British colonialists, i.e. developing Singapore into a flourishing trading station. He got rid of the island's greatest plague, the rats, by paying a cash sum for every dead rat, and to prevent racial conflict, he settled the various racial groups in separate quarters. Chinatown, Little India and the district around Arab Street owe their distinctive character to Raffles. His own residence was built on the present fort at Canning Hill, where he felt that the fresh breeze blowing in off the sea was good for his fragile health.

Raffle's private life was far from happy. His first wife, apparently the ex-lover of his superior, passed away shortly after their marriage and all four children from his second marriage died at an early age, three of them probably succumbing to malaria. Raffles himself died just one day before his 45th birthday. Even the flower that was named after him does not do him justice. Rafflesia is a parasitic plant that smells of putrid meat.

Lee Kuan Yew

When, on 16 September 1923, a boy by the name of Lee Kuan Yew was born into wealthy Chinese family, no one imagined that the boy would one day lead the island's government, let alone become the longest-serving prime minster in the world. However, the boy's parents were clearly not without ambition for their bright son, as they also called him Harry and had him educated according to the English model, something that could only be of benefit to his professional career, given the circumstances of colonial rule.

He went to grammar school and studied at Raffles College. In September 1946, one year after the Japanese surrender, Harry Lee Kuan Yew, then aged 23, went to Cambridge to study law. He gained a double first and was admitted to the English bar in 1950. That same year he met a young Singaporean woman, Kwa Geok Ghoo, who had also studied at Cambridge and was later to become his wife. Instead of practising as a barrister in England, he returned to Singapore, where he was soon appointed legal adviser to the Postal Union. He set about learning Mandarin and became politically active, joining with like-minded young professionals to campaign for an end to colonial rule.

The People's Action Party (PAP) was founded with Lee Kuan Yew as its general secretary. Even though at times Lee co-operated with some of the more radical opponents of British colonial rule, namely the Communist Party, he was always a fanatical anti-communist. In 1958, Lee helped to negotiate for Singapore the status of self-governing state within the Commonwealth. Elections were held in May 1959, with Lee campaigning on an anti-colonialist, anti-communist platform. On 5 June, the newly-elected prime minister Lee Kuan Yew announced that he and his ministers had taken over the running of all internal affairs. The English yoke had finally been shaken off.

Some refer to him respectfully as 'Mr Singapore', others less deferentially, but still affectionately, as 'Uncle Harry'. The Chinese liked to describe him as a banana: yellow on the outside, white on the inside. Nevertheless, his self-discipline and successful battle against corruption remain an example to other rulers. Singapore without Lee Kuan Yew seems impossible to imagine. What about Lee Kuan Yew without Singapore? He was once asked whether he regarded himself as Chinese: 'Ethnically, I am certainly Chinese, but otherwise I am a Singaporean'.

Inside the OUB Centre
Preceding pages: the Singapore
skyline at night

Route 1

On the trail of Raffles – the ★★ Colonial District

To fully appreciate this tour of Singapore's colonial past – the Civic and Cultural District – visitors will need a whole day. In the heart of the modern city stand impressive monuments from the 19th century which testify to the prosperity of the former British trading post. Alongside the towering steel and glass office blocks, some of which reach a height of 280m (920ft), the grandiose colonial-style architecture looks modest but nevertheless solid. An ascent of one of the skyscrapers, included in the route, provides a magnificent panoramic view of much of Singapore. To fit in a tour of the National Museum, set out in good time, preferably by 9am.

Raffles Place

Raffles Place is a small, green oasis set between the huge office blocks of the Central Business District on the Singapore River's southern bank. Passers-by often take a break on the square's neatly-trimmed lawn while, underneath, lies the cavernous Raffles Place underground station, one of the busiest on the network.

To the west, the rectangular square is bordered by the acute-angled 280-m (920-ft) tall **OUB Centre ❶**, designed by well-known Japanese architect Kenzo Tange. Lofty views are no more to be had from its former 60th floor restaurant called the Pinnacle, a victim of the increasing demand for premium office space.

A panoramic view of the city is, however, available free on the other side of Chulia Street by the banks of the Singapore River. The equally tall and also Kenzo Tange-designed **★★ UOB Plaza** boasts an expensive Chinese restaurant on the 60th floor (**Top of the Plaza**, tel: 538

32 32). Since not everyone who enjoys stunning views can afford to pay similarly stunning prices for food, take the lift to the 37th floor **Sky Lobby** for free views over the northern side of the city. A distinguishing feature of the ground floor courtyard area is the nearly 4-m (13-ft) tall *Homage to Newton* sculpture, a Salvador Dali replica.

Follow the river downstream as far as **Cavenagh Bridge**. To the right of this iron suspension bridge (built in 1869) is the colonial **Fullerton Building**, built by the British in 1928 as the **General Post Office** and still in operation. Entrance is via Battery Road to the right.

On the other side of the bridge, it is impossible to miss the palatial ★ **Empress Place Building ❷** that dates from 1854. It was originally used as the courthouse and then it became the offices for the emigration and immigration authorities. The building was restored in 1989 to house a museum for Asiatic culture. The museum was closed in 1995 and a new museum of Asian civilisation is expected to take its place in 1997. Hopefully, some of the many old-fashioned (empty) safes inside that once contained official documents will be on display. One thing that certainly will not be open to the public is the mysterious **time capsule**, which is kept beneath a glass pyramid outside the entrance. The capsule is due to be opened in 2015 when Singapore celebrates 50 years of indepedence.

Cavenagh Bridge

The mysterious time capsule

21

ROUTE 1

0   500 m

Parliament House

A few yards from the riverbank stands a tall white **obelisk** which was built by the colonial rulers during 1850 in honour of the Indian governor, Dalhousie. It marks the start of a pretty avenue which leads directly to the dark, bronze **Raffles Statue**. Unveiled in 1887, the sculpture is just one of the many tributes to the founder of Singapore.

It is set against the backdrop of the **Victoria Concert Hall and Theatre ❸**, the home of the Singapore Symphony Orchestra, and the island's premier venue for opera and ballet.

Follow the narrow lane that passes to the left of the concert hall as far as Parliament Lane. This leads directly up to **Parliament House** (1827), whose iron gate conceals huge, light-grey stone columns. This structure, which was originally planned as a private residence, is now used as the debating chamber for the Singapore parliament, but it is not open to the public. It was planned by the architect George Coleman who was responsible for several of Singapore's notable buildings.

Another ★ **statue** of Sir Stamford Raffles stands at the point where Parliament Lane meets the bank of the Singapore River, but this one is gleaming white. This spot is known as the **Raffles Landing Site** as it was here on 29 January 1819 that the city's founder first set foot on Singaporean soil. On the opposite side of the river lies the ★★ **Boat Quay**, a complex with many restaurants and bars which was restored during the 1980s. The former shophouses with their tiny ground-floor workshops were once home to more rats than people. Now the pulsating nightlife goes on until the early hours.

For a fascinating excursion along the ★★ **Singapore River**, take one of the so-called *bumboats* which depart from the Landing Site (daily 9am–10pm; departures on the hour). The boat trips first head upstream beneath the

Skyscrapers dominate Boat Quay
Raffles Landing Site

low bridges as far as the **Ord Bridge**, where there was once a Malay village. They then turn round and sail down to the mouth of the river where the symbol for Singapore, the half-lion, half-fish ★ **Merlion** *(see page 5)* is a popular subject for amateur photographers. The recorded commentary describes in detail the history of the trading post. It also explains the original function of the wooden *bumboats*. They were employed to carry goods from the vessels anchored in the harbour to the warehouses further up the river. Mention is also made of how the quality of the water has changed: the river was once a foul-smelling sewer!

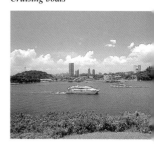

Merlion – half-lion, half-fish
Cruising boats

Go back down Parliament Lane to High Street. About 10metres further on to the left, before the narrow north front of Parliament House, a black **miniature elephant** with white tusks stands on a stone plinth. This fine-looking statue was a gift to Singapore from the King of Siam during an official visit on 16 March 1871. Diagonally opposite the statue lies the **Padang**, or 'field' as the Malay word is translated. In the colonial era, sports, games, military parades and social events were held here. This grassy area, the size of several football pitches, is still used for public occasions, including the annual celebration of the country's independence. Take a good look at the **Singapore Cricket Club** club-house. This building (1852) that houses the elite club is a fine example of the colonial architectural style found throughout the tropics. The faded charm within can only be imagined, as it is closed to tourists. At the north end of the Padang, the cream of Singaporean society meets in the **Singapore Recreation Club**.

A number of splendid edifices can be seen on the other side of **St Andrew's Street**. As public buildings, they are open to the visitors. The first one is the ★ **Supreme Court**. This classical building with a facade of stout Corinthian columns projects a sense of dignity. Dating from 1939, it is one of the last colonial constructions built in the city. Only a little older but no less impressive is the huge flight of steps beneath the colonnade of the next monumental structure: the ★ **City Hall**. Finished in 1929, it was the setting for the public surrender of the Japanese after World War II.

Built in 1863, the gleaming white ★ **St Andrew's Cathedral** ❹ is a major landmark. The biggest church in Singapore, its interior is modestly decorated: white-washed walls and a few stained-glass windows behind the altar. It is, nevertheless, ideal not only for quiet contemplation but also as a cool refuge from the tropical heat.

Coleman Street, named after the creative and highly-regarded architect mentioned above, leads into the heart of one of the city's shopping quarters. On the right is the **Peninsula Plaza**, on the left the **Peninsula Shopping**

St Andrew's Cathedral

Centre; and there are a number of places nearby to enjoy a fortifying drink before starting out on the arduous climb that lies ahead.

First cross the broad Hill Street and enter the pleasantly cool **Armenian Church of St Gregory ❺**. This small, apostolic chapel (1837) with a roof constructed by Coleman, is the oldest church in Singapore. As the Armenian community has declined, services rarely take place in this simple, sacred building.

Coleman Street now climbs gently and becomes the steeper Canning Rise which winds its way up ★★ **Fort Canning Hill**. Behind the Registry of Marriages lies **Fort Canning Park**, with its large areas of well-tended grass.

Entrance to the Spice Garden

Just to the right is the **Spice Garden ❻** and it is worth stopping here for a few minutes to enjoy the scents. This is a miniature version of the 19-hectare (47-acre) garden that Raffles laid out in 1822 on what was then Government Hill. He wanted to find out which spices grew well in the tropical heat of Singapore. Many, such as cloves and nutmeg, thrived. These discoveries brought riches to Singapore until the middle of the 19th century. Exotic spices were as precious as gold, and every European maritime power sought to gain control over this profitable trade.

Cross the Spice Garden and pass through the weathered, stone arch to the **Christian cemetery** with its 600 or so graves. The gravestones have been removed and bedded into the perimeter wall. Although the inscriptions are difficult to read, they describe the tragic fate that befell many Chinese and European Christians who were laid to rest here during the 19th century and the name of the architect Coleman appears once again. His tombstone shows the year of his death as 1841.

Fort Canning Centre

Climb a stone staircase up to the **Fort Canning Centre ❼**, where the **Singapore Dance Theatre** trains and rehearses. Another flight of stairs behind the building leads up to the sparse remains of **Fort Canning**. It was built by the British between 1859 and 1861 as a fortification and consists of an arms store, hospital and barracks. Its construction involved levelling off an area of about 3 hectares (7 acres) at the summit. However, the thick walls were demolished in 1926 and, apart from an old stone gate, there is little to see. Enjoy a few minutes of peace in the shadow of some large fig trees. Only the cheerful bird songs and the screeching of the cicadas interrupt the silence.

A well-signposted circular tour branches off at the old stone gate to the higher **Fort Canning Reservoir**, which affords some attractive views over the city. The path passes some historic plaques and ancient, iron cannons – but none of them originated from the old fort. Just before the path arrives back at the **Fort Canning Centre**, on the hillside to the right, lies the **Keramat Iskandar Shah ❽**, a richly-

decorated tombstone. The Malays still honour Sultan
Megat Iskandar Shah, who founded Melaka at the beginning of the 15th century. For Malays, the hill is sacred.
They call it the **Forbidden Hill**, but Raffles disregarded
their feelings.

A well-earned break

Descend through the Christian cemetery and then pass
through the left-hand stone arch. Fort Canning Rise leads
down to Fort Canning Road. The ★★ **National Museum
and Art Gallery** (Tuesday to Sunday 9am–5.30pm;
nearest MRT station: Dhoby Ghaut) is situated to the right
at the junction with Stamford Road. Built in 1887 in classical style, the building with its green shutters actually
resembles an official residence. It contains many items
of interest relating to the history, ethnology and archae-
ology of Southeast Asia, and Singapore in particular. Some
real treasures are to be found among the jade exhibits,
which were endowed by the 'Tiger Balm brothers' Aw
Boon Haw and Aw Boon Par. A full tour of the museum,
which should include the adjoining art gallery where the
work of contemporary Asian artists is displayed, will take
at least an hour and a half.

25

The trishaw alternative

Although trishaw drivers wait over the road for tired
tourists, continue on foot along Stamford Road and past
the **National Library**.

The **National Museum Shop** ⑩ *(see Shopping, page
81)* at No 53 Armenian Street is a short detour to the right.
This store sells many attractive souvenirs and informative
books on the history of Singapore. A detour to the left into
Queen Street leads to the impressive **Cathedral of the
Good Shepherd**. Designed by Dennis McSwiney, a pupil
of George Coleman, it was completed in 1846. Opposite,
the new **Singapore Art Museum** ⑪ (Tuesday to Sunday
9am–5pm) occupies what was **St Joseph's Institution**,
the city's first Roman Catholic church. Contemporary
art from Southeast Asia is now displayed here.

View from the Westin Stamford

Raffles Hotel

26

Return to Stamford Road. Before reaching the **Capitol Theatre** cinema on the corner, look for the designer clothes displayed in several of the small, but unusual boutiques. Diagonally opposite (and impossible to miss) is the gleaming, silver shopping palace known as **Raffles City**. To cool down and relax, make for this elegant air-conditioned complex with its two hotels. One of Singapore's most-photographed prospects can be enjoyed from the expensive ★ **Compass Rose** restaurant in the **Westin Stamford Hotel**. The view is not quite so impressive from the bar, also on the 70th floor (218m/715ft) – hence the cheaper prices. It is possible to look down into War Memorial Park on the other side of Beach Road where the **Cenotaph**, a monument more popularly known as Chopsticks, commemorates those who fell in World War II.

Leave Raffles City by the Bras Basah Road exit, cross the road and there stands the gleaming white ★★★ **Raffles Hotel** ⑫. When examined at close quarters, the walls clearly do not date from the colonial era. This luxurious hotel was re-opened in 1991 after two years of comprehensive renovation and the addition of new annexes. It all started in 1887 when two Armenian brothers, the Sarkies, converted a few rooms into a simple hotel. Now the guests stay in grand suites and non-residents swell the crowds attracted to the hotel by the two-storey arcade with its array of expensive boutiques, jewellers, art dealers, designers, top-class restaurants and bars *(see Food and Drink, page 77)*. Non-residents may enter the hotel, but access to the guests' lounges is not permitted – it is only possible to look in from the outside. The atmosphere in the famous 'Grand Old Lady of the East', as the wealthy 19th-century travellers called it, can be sampled in the reception hall (entrance in Beach Road). Follow Rudyard Kipling's example and enjoy a Singapore Sling *(see page 77)* in the Writers' Bar.

Leave the hotel by the main entrance, turn right and follow Beach Road. At the next junction turn left into Raffles Boulevard. On the left-hand side stands **Suntech City**, an ultra-modern convention hall.

★ **Marina Square** with its four hotels is the island's largest shopping centre. The **Marina Mandarin** boasts the biggest atrium in Southeast Asia and the **Pan Pacific** has a glass lift, from which diners can survey the city as they rise to the **Hai Tien Lo** restaurant. **Esplanade Park** between Marina Square and Marina Bay is currently being converted into the **Singapore Performing Arts Centre**. When completed in the year 2000, the centre, occupying prime position at the mouth of the Singapore River, will be the cultural hub of Singapore theatre and the arts.

The City Hall MRT Station is only a short distance away.

Function at the Marina Mandarin

Route 2

★★★ Orchard Road

The Singaporeans' enthusiasm for shopping is encapsu-
lated in the expression 'Shop 'til you drop'. At some time
or other, everyone will probably feel like dropping when
on a shopping excursion through the multi-storey malls of
Orchard Road: it may be fatigue or it may be the prices
that the international designers and couturiers demand.
Orchard Road is no place for bargain hunters, but window
shoppers will derive pleasure from the stylishly-decorated
displays. Despite the vastness of the shopping areas, the
range of merchandise is less wide than one might imagine.

Shop 'til you drop

Shoppers will certainly not succumb to the heat, as the
stores are all air-conditioned – sometimes the temperature
controls are set just a little too low. Well-stocked food stalls
and supermarkets in the basements will take care of any
hunger pangs.

The Orchard Road shops start on a fairly modest scale
by the **Dhoby Ghaut** MRT station. On the left-hand side
by Penang Road lies **Park Mall**, which attracts many
house-proud Singaporeans with shops specialising in designer furniture, light fixtures and other home furnishings.
On the Orchard Road side, the ageing **Plaza Singapura**
⓭ has lost customers to more swanky malls further up
the street. The shops here specialise in sports and electrical goods, musical instruments and household equip-
ment. Follow the right-hand side of Orchard Road past the
well-protected entrance to **Istana**, the president's palace.
The palace lies in parkland, hidden away behind thick vegetation, and the neatly dressed guards will not allow unau-
thorised visitors to the site.

27

Stylish displays

Duty-free goods are for sale a few yards further down the road in the basement of the **Duty Free Shop** (DFS) in the **Le Meridien Hotel**. The place is usually inundated with Japanese tour groups, who are often in a hurry. Duty-free goods are only obtainable on the production of an onward flight ticket.

There is nothing fashionable about **Orchard Plaza** , but to compensate, the prices in these overflowing souvenir, shoe and textile shops are very reasonable. The Goh Kin Camera Service on the 2nd floor provides a rapid camera repair service.

Centrepoint

The **Singapore Post Philatelic Bureau** on the other side of the busy road is a must for stamp collectors (*see Shopping, pages 81*).

Continue on the right-hand side of Orchard Road and **Orchard Point** 🕒 is the next shopping centre. The four-storey building is modern and spacious inside. Some interesting antique shops can be found on the top floor.

Back outside amid the hurly-burly of hurrying shoppers, take a right turn into **Cuppage Road**. This quickly leads to ★ **Cuppage Terrace** *(see Nightlife, page 82)*, a busy square surrounded by bars, restaurants and snack bars. This is a favourite haunt of Singapore's large expatriate community.

Peranakan Place

One of the busiest and most attractive shopping centres is **Centrepoint** 🕕. Even the escalators are trimmed with gold. The tastefully decorated branches of famous fashion designers are spread throughout the four floors. But other, less exclusive stores such as Marks & Spencer and Robinsons occupy several floors. Large bookshops such as **MPH** and **Times The Bookshop** stock a good range of English language books and magazines.

★★ **Peranakan Place**, a little further on, is also very popular with tourists. On the one hand, it is possible to watch the hustle and bustle of Orchard Road over a beer in one of the street cafés, on the other hand, it is one way of appreciating Peranakan architecture (*see page 9*).

Follow ★ **Emerald Hill Road** ⓱ uphill for a short distance, looking out for the extravagantly restored, two-storey dwellings of the old Peranakan population. Many have now been converted into agencies, offices and restaurants.

Emerald Hill facades

Several sports clothing shops and a number of well-stocked watch and clock shops, specialising in the colourful Swatch brands, can be found in the adjoining **Orchard Emerald Shopping Centre** ⓲.

The **John Little** department store in the **Specialist's Shopping Centre** ⓳ on the other side of Orchard Road is renowned, among other things, for its large selection of fabrics.

Several multi-storey shops now follow closely on the right-hand side of the road. There is the rather charmless **Midpoint Orchard** and then **Orchard Shopping Centre**. Probably only **OG Orchard** ⓴ with its exquisite fashion outlets deserves a closer examination. The brand new five-storey shoppers' paradise **The Heeren** ㉑ is also worth exploring.

29

Expensive, international fashion designers are housed strictly according to status in the smart **Paragon Shopping Centre** ㉒. At the very top is the **Metro** department store, while in the basement the **Sogo** chain has established a lavishly stocked supermarket. Freshly prepared and reasonably priced *sushi* are among its attractions (*see page 76*).

Paragon Shopping Centre

In the **Promenade Shopping Centre** ㉓, the displays – principally the work of young Asian fashion designers – are a touch more elegant. They can be seen from a moving walkway that climbs in a spiral.

Vintage models on display

Ngee Ann City

On the other side of the street, the ★★ **Ngee Ann City** ❷❹ is an even larger and smarter shopping citadel. The two towers are occupied, both above and below ground, by the branches of over 70 respected fashion designers. Other large department stores such as **Takashimaya** and **Harrods** are based here. Look out for the shop that sells souvenirs of the Eastern & Oriental Express, while Basement B2 is an absolute must for gourmets. A post office is located on the fourth floor.

The facade of the adjacent **Wisma Atria** ❷❺ looks rather modest by comparison, but the interior consists of neat galleries with small but attractive shops selling unusual fashions and fashion accessories. By contrast, the Japanese **Isetan** department store sells a wide range of cheap, mass-produced goods. In the basement near the entrance to the Orchard MRT station, a subway leads under the road towards Scotts Road and **Tangs** ❷❻, Singapore's busiest department store. When Tangs holds a sale that promises genuine bargains, it attracts the Singapore public in droves.

As the yawning gaps indicate, many of the local traders have left the neighbouring **Lucky Plaza**. They gave up trying to entice tourists into their photography, luggage and jewellery shops by claiming huge price reductions. Haggling is perfectly acceptable here, but shoppers should be wary, as there are some unscrupulous traders about.

A detour along Scotts Road passes some of the city's finest hotels (Marriott, Hyatt, etc). More elegant shopping centres lie beyond. In **Scotts** ❷❼, for example, the shops specialise in cosmetics and fashions for young people.

Ready for a drink? On the right-hand side, just a few yards further on, is the ★★ **Goodwood Park Hotel**, formerly known as the 'Teutonia Club', the meeting place for the German community before World War I. 'High tea' which consists of a wide selection of sandwiches and cakes is available in L'Espresso between 2.30 and 6.30pm.

Goodwood Park Hotel

Pacific Plaza ❷❽, just opposite Scotts, is another attractive shopping centre. Take a look at the huge selection of CDs on the top floor. Next door at the junction of Orchard and Scotts roads is the **Shaw Centre**, housing another **Isetan** department store and the massive **Lido** cineplex featuring the latest films.

Lane Crawford

Cross over to the huge glass complex belonging to the Hong Kong-based ★ **Lane Crawford** department store ❷❾. It is well worth spending a little time in this store looking through the quality goods on sale, as prices are often reduced quite dramatically.

Liat Towers ❸❿ on the same side of Orchard Road previously housed a miniature replica of the French department store *Galerie Lafayette*, now closed for the second time at the same premises. **The Far East Shopping Cen-**

tre **31** with its narrow walkways and little shops is clearly one of Singapore's older shopping centres. Tailors offer their services with typical Asian aplomb, but there are also jewellers, opticians, camera shops and antique sellers.

The next building combines the **Hilton Hotel** and a shopping arcade that leads through to Orchard Boulevard and the **Four Seasons** Hotel. With numerous children's clothes shops and a multi-national toy chain, **Forum – The Shopping Mall 32** has set its sights firmly on the younger generation, but there are also one or two fine fashion boutiques for adults.

Forum

On the left-hand side, where Orchard Road becomes **Tanglin Road**, is a branch of the famous **Jim Thompson's**. The main attractions here are the unusual fashion accessories made from magnificent Thai silk. The **Tanglin Shopping Centre 33** recently underwent a facelift and it has since lost some of its special atmosphere, but it is still renowned for its made-to-measure tailoring. The **China Silk House** on level 2 has a wide selection of flowing Chinese silks.

Fashionable accessories

Tastefully imitating the English country house style is the former **Tanglin Place** department store **34**, now awaiting new tenants. The **Tudor Court** next door is attractive, as is the **Tanglin Mall 35**. Here, a good mixture of outlets selling their wares at sensible prices are enticing shoppers away from Orchard Road.

31

On the other side of Tanglin Road, pass the **Duty Free Shop** (DFS), where rows of buses are always waiting to pick up groups of shopping-mad Japanese tourists. This store sells expensive goods with reputable brand names, but they are not appreciably cheaper than anywhere else in Singapore. The white-tiled facade of the **Delfi Orchard 36** gleams brightly at the junction with Orchard Road. Chrome and glass cannot conceal the fact that many of the spaces are vacant. In the merciless fight for customers, this shopping mall has been on the losing side. Between the gaps, a few furniture shops and jewellers have survived.

Orchard Towers 37 is different. The appetising smells emanating from the food stalls in the basement attract scores of shoppers. **Miss Ming** on the first floor sells chic and well-made ladies fashions in Thai silk.

Palais Renaissance 38 next door was built with the luxury market in mind, but it always looks deserted. It is further proof that Singapore's retailers cannot rely solely on the purchasing power of the city's wealthy 10,000.

Mural on Orchard Road

Seemingly unperturbed by the rampant consumerism in the vicinity, the dignified **Thai embassy** enjoys an idyllic spot within a fenced off garden. Just next door, it is business as usual in the shops of the **International Building 39** on Orchard Road. The Orchard MRT station is just across the road.

Shophouse facades

Route 3

★★★ Chinatown

This tour is an introduction to the Chinese side of Singapore – or rather what is left of the vitality of the city's Asian quarter now that all the furious restoration work is complete. Sadly, much of the colourful and noisy chaos generated by the enthusiastic salesmen and artisans has disappeared. On the plus side, sewage no longer runs down the gutters at the roadside and damp and musty smells no longer emanate from inside the dilapidated shophouses.

The old Chinese quarter that Raffles established has spruced itself up and is now stealing the limelight from other parts of Singapore. But do not expect to find anything exotic – there are no opium dens and no unhygienic food stalls. What is on display in Singapore is really 'Chinatown for Beginners': immaculately restored streets with shophouses painted in pastel shades, tidy shops and appetising restaurants. But a walk through the maze of narrow alleys and past the lively market stalls will still provide a glimpse of the original Chinatown. Allow about six hours for the full tour.

Sri Mariamman Temple

There is an Indian temple in the heart of Chinatown! The ★★ **Sri Mariamman Temple** ❹ with its smooth white exterior walls makes a strange starting point for this tour. It is situated on South Bridge Road between Pagoda Street and Temple Street and can be reached either by taxi or by a Singapore trolley. It is impossible to miss the brightly-coloured pyramid of deities above the main entrance – a characteristic feature of Hindu temples. The pairs of shoes by the entrance give a clear message: visitors may only enter barefoot. This is the oldest temple in Singapore, and it is dedicated to the goddess Mariamman. It was built in 1827 by a wealthy merchant, initially out of wood but it was later restored with stone.

Diagonally opposite the temple is a traditional chemist's shop, ★ **Eu Yan Sang** (239 South Bridge Road; Monday to Saturday 8.30am–6pm) supplies the Chinese with the exotic herbs that are supposed to cure every kind of minor ailment. Even if some Chinese have little faith in their own medicine, they furtively glance inside where they can read about ginseng and all the other herbal cures, and can inhale the aromatic perfumes. On sale here are birds' nests. To the Chinese, the birds' saliva that holds the nests together is a protein-rich delicacy.

Follow South Bridge Road to the south and then turn left at the next corner into a small, gently climbing road called **Ann Siang Hill**. On the right-hand side stands a tastefully restored, three-storey building with gleaming, green roof tiles. When it rains, the water pours down and creates a kind of curtain around the house. This is no accident, as the Chinese believe that the rain curtain helps to 'keep money within'.

Peace in a bustling quarter

A few yards further on the left is **Club Street**, so-called because of the numerous club houses that the various dialect groups set up here in the early part of the 19th century. These centres were important in helping to get new arrivals established. Only a few of these club houses, now known as 'associations', have survived. In their place behind renovated facades, traditional hotels such as the **Damenlou Hotel** (*see Accommodation, page 95*), have opened up. For safety reasons, nearly all the entrances have had to adopt the simple doors required by the Singaporean government as part of the facelift. Visually, they may be preferable, but they do not fit in with the Chinese love of bright colours and rich ornamentation.

Chinese love bright colours

Many house owners changed after the restoration work had been completed. They either lacked the financial means to maintain the property or else they were unable to prove ownership, since, in the past, property had only been handed down by word of mouth. In many cases, the government acquired the crumbling buildings for a very small sum, safe in the knowledge that restored real estate in Chinatown could be leased out for huge sums.

With the high rents that are now due, more and more of the houses are being used by traders, advertising agencies, sound studios and the legal profession. In the evening when the offices close, the streets, that once throbbed with life round the clock, are peaceful. At the end of Club Street, continue over Cross Street and carry straight on along **China Street**, but take a wander down the narrow side lanes. The old shophouses have either been splendidly restored or else they wait with the cats and rats for the builders to arrive.

Inside Wak Hai Cheng Bio

At the end of China Street, turn right into the busy **Church Street**. Cross over at the nearest pedestrian lights and then turn left into the narrow **Phillip Street**. On the corner stand the weathered walls of the ★★ **Wak Hai Cheng Bio Temple** ❹. It was built in 1826 by the Teochew community shortly after their arrival in Singapore as a gesture of thanksgiving for their safe sea journey. The surrounding area contrasts starkly with the modern skyscrapers by the business quarter around the Singapore River.

On **Telok Ayer Street** (left-hand side) a new **Food Centre** has opened up to cater for the Central Business District workers. On the right-hand side is the site of the old Fuk Tak Chi Temple which was completely demolished and not replaced when the houses were given their facelift. On the right by the corner of **Boon Tat Street** stands the **Nagore Durgha Shrine** ❷. Its facade of columns and towers is an architectural compendium. Moslems from southern India worship at the shrine which is the burial site of Shahul Hamid Nagore, one of the great personalities in Moslem culture.

Thian Hock Keng

To the rear stands the richly decorated entrance to the ★★ **Thian Hock Keng Temple**, the oldest and most interesting of all the temples in Singapore. A *joss house*, as the little altars were known, stood here as early as 1821.

It had been built by immigrants from Fukien Province for Ma Chu Po, the 'patron saint' of mariners. At that time, the harbour was only a short distance away but, because so much land has since been reclaimed from the sea, it is now well inland. The present, spacious site dates from 1841, when the Chinese, who were prospering in Singapore, were able to afford tiles from Holland and wrought iron from Scotland.

Thian Hock Keng

Only a few yards further on, but easily missed, stands the third sacred building on Telok Ayer Street: the modest **Al Abrar Mosque** which was built by Moslem Indians in 1855.

Enough of holy places. The sizzling food stands at the next junction are sure to turn the mind to more worldly requirements. After a bite to eat and some welcome refreshments turn right into McCallum Street. A *joss house* at the end is open to the devout.

Local vegetable store

Make a short detour to the right into **Amoy Street**. Renovation work has finished and the smart premises are now being snapped up by the business community. At the corner of Amoy Street and McCallum Street, a narrow, unnamed alley passes to the right of the *joss house* and a flight of steps leads up to **Ann Siang Road**.

Turn left towards a number of lavishly and lovingly restored houses. These show clearly that lessons have been learnt from the first unimaginative attempts at wholesale renovation. In the middle of **Erskine Road**'s monotonous row of houses, a turning on the right leads to an unusual hotel, the **Inn of Sixth Happiness** (*see Accommodation, page 95*). Continue along Kadayanallur Street, which soon joins the wide **Maxwell Road**. On the right-hand side is another **Food Centre**.

On the other side of Maxwell Road, the pedestrian-only ★ **Murray Terrace** ❹ or Food Alley is devoted almost entirely to restaurants *(see Food and Drink pages 71–8)*. A large board provides a key to each restaurant and the type of food it serves.

Cut through to **Tanjong Pagar Road** via **Cook Street**. The three-storey shophouses here were renovated some time ago and they now house attractive, new shops with colourful shutters. Beware of the foot reflex massage that is offered at No 22 (and other places). Anyone not used to having the reflex zones on their feet massaged vigorously may find the process extremely painful.

A signpost indicates the route to ★ **Duxton Hill**, a fully-restored quarter now home to Singapore's smart set. Take a stroll up and down Duxton Road, past all the beautiful shops, western-style bars and the elegant **Duxton Hotel**.

On the right-hand side, at a point on Duxton Hill where there are cobblestones between the houses and the decorative cultivated areas, a passageway cuts through to Neil

Windows on the world

Road (11am–9pm only). Look out for the wide glass door beneath '51 Neil Road'. This passage leads into the ★ **Tanjong Pagar Heritage** ㊹, a long complex of buildings to which 16 shophouses were linked. As well as several shops, there is also an interesting exhibition about the early 19th-century fishing village of **Tanjong Pagar**. Its Malay inhabitants were called *Orang Laut* or, roughly translated, 'the sea nomads'.

Local news

Enter Neil Road through the main gateway and then turn right. Many of the restored premises in the arcades are now either 'eating houses' – simple restaurants – or 'tea houses' e.g. **Yixing Xuan** (23 Neil Road, tel: 224 6961) with its large selection of teacups and teapots, and **Tea Chapter** (9A–11A Neil Road, tel: 226 1175).

Tea urn

The Chinese do not just drink tea, they celebrate it, whether at home or in the special tea houses that offer a wide variety of teas. Yellow tea is the most expensive, green tea the cheapest. The temperature of the water is the decisive factor. It should reach a temperature of 95°C/203°F, but not boil. Experts rely on their sense of hearing, laymen watch for a cherry-sized bubble to rise up from the base of the glass jug. Then the water is hot enough to warm up the tiny teapot, before it can be filled half full with tea leaves. The first infusion cleans the tea. Then the tea is left to brew for 30 seconds before the almost clear liquid is poured into slender, porcelain cups about the same size as a sherry glass. Do not start to drink yet, though. First take a sniff and absorb the aroma. The tea is drunk from tiny porcelain bowls. They must be brought up to the mouth between thumb, forefinger and middle finger. A barbarian will drink his cup in one sip, but the Chinese take three. Now on to the next round. The tea leaves can be re-used up to five more times, but for each new brew, the water must infuse for an extra 10 minutes. Spicy 'tea eggs' are served as snacks. These are hard-boiled in tea-flavoured water (*see Shopping, page 81*).

Follow Neil Road northward and into **South Bridge Road**, passing some tall, unsightly residential blocks. Until the 1960s, Sago Lane was where elderly, childless Chinese came to die, but the area has since been flattened to make way for new buildings.

Shops on the left in **Sago Street** sell traditional Chinese goods, e.g. Chinese healing oil (No 16). On the left-hand side, steps lead up to the ★★ **Chinatown Complex** ㊺, a chaotic, but fascinating Chinese market stalls here sell not just clothes and household goods etc, but also, on the upper floor, typical Chinese fare: sea cucumbers, fish heads, black-spiced eggs, live frogs and turtles.

Take a stroll through modern Chinatown. Since the renovation work was completed, many new tourist-orientated souvenir shops have opened up. Formerly the various tradesmen such as tailors and basket-makers were clustered together in **Trengganu Street**, **Smith Street** and **Temple Street**.

A popular souvenir

The ★ **Chinaman Scholar Gallery** ㊻ (14B Trengganu Street; daily 9am–4pm) is worth a visit. It is a small museum with exhibits that date from the early days of Chinatown. This narrow but deep (16-m/50-ft) shophouse, built in 1890, illustrates the living conditions of the Chinese middle classes at that time. Above the shop lived the parents (and in some cases the husband had a second wife), while the children lived on the second floor, even after they had married.

Turn left into **Pagoda Street** and then left into South Bridge Road. Only a few yards further on stands the ★ **Jamae Mosque** ㊾ where, since 1835, southern Indians have worshipped the tomb of a saint.

Turn down **Mosque Street** to reach the multi-storey shopping centres that are favoured by the local people. Two footbridges cross the busy New Bridge Road and Eu Tong Sen Street.

37

The ★★ **People's Park Complex** ㊽ on the left comprises several floors and has a bewilderingly colourful array of shops selling jewellery, leather goods, fabrics and hi-fis. But do not expect to find any special bargains here or at the **People's Park Centre** (nearest MRT station: Outram) nearby. Cheap and cheerful food stalls in the centre's basement stay busy for most of the day, creating a lively atmosphere. If time and stamina permit, shopaholics can cross from the northern end into **Chinatown Point** via a covered footbridge. The architects who worked on this project tried hard to create a stylish environment for shoppers. Chrome and glass predominate around spiral walkways lined with attractive shops. The goods on offer are unusual and of high quality, but not cheap.

Chinatown Point
Sago Street

Route 4

★★ Little India

Visitors to Singapore who follow their noses will eventually find themselves in Little India – led there by the powerful aroma of curry and other exotic spices that seems to permeate the whole of this fascinating quarter. But Little India is also a feast for the eyes. Saris interwoven with gold thread, shimmering silk on display in the fabric stores

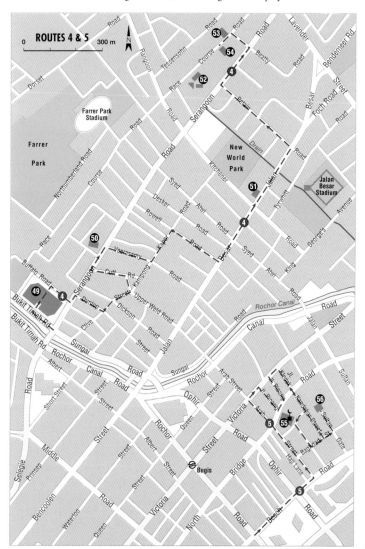

ROUTES 4 & 5
0   300 m

The Zhujiao Centre

and glittering gems and precious metals in the jewellery shops. The taste buds will also be in for a treat, as no food is more strongly spiced than that of southern India. Allow three hours to be swept away into the exotic world of the Indian sub-continent. Start in the morning because in the late afternoon there is a risk that the Buddhist temples will be closed.

Little India is also the focus of Hindu festivals (*see pages 67–9*). Those lucky enough to be in Singapore during Deepavali, the Hindu New Year, will find Little India a riot of lights, lamps and garlands. Rather more macabre is Thaipusam, a two-day period of atonement when people may wear skewers through their flesh.

Serangoon Road is the main artery in Little India. This tour begins in the south on the corner with Bukit Timah Road. The relatively modern ★★ **Zhujiao Centre** ㊾ is a multi-storey maze of colourful market stalls. The sight of goldsmiths selling their ornate ear-rings, chains and bracelets is reminiscent of a scene from *A Thousand and One Nights*. Prices vary from day to day as the price of gold fluctuates. A chart in every shop gives the price per gram of the worked gold.

Serangoon Road

A tour up, down and around is like a voyage of discovery: there are fabric sellers, shoemakers, food stands and little stalls where garlands are made for visitors to the temple. And remember to pay a visit to the **Wet Market** in the basement. This section, which overflows with vegetables, fish and meat, gets its name from the hosepipes that, in line with Singapore regulations, constantly spray the floor with water. And lingering as a backdrop to everything else is the pervasive aroma of the hot spices that are used to flavour Indian curries.

At the rear of the complex ★ **Buffalo Road** runs parallel to Bukit Timah Road. During the first 30 years of this

Shady characters

39

Sri Veeramakaliamman Temple
Hindu images

Inside Sri Veeramakaliamman

century, *kerbau* (the Malay word for cattle) grazed here, but the Indian immigrants later turned the district into a trading quarter, specialising in buying and selling gold. However, the furious pace of Singaporean change has not spared Little India either. The favoured approach here was not so much to simply maintain the old buildings, but to renovate them in the old style – all financed by higher rents. As a result, most of the long-established jewellery shops moved into the Zhujiao Centre. A quick tour round the quarter will reveal that, in fact, many streets have been left to decay. And in Singapore that means only one thing: pull it down and start again.

Follow Buffalo Road as far as Serangoon Road and then turn left. Trade keeps everyone busy on this lively thoroughfare. The windows of the shops where the Indian women buy the material for their saris are piled high with brightly coloured rolls of fabric. The same shops fit little girls with frilly pastel-coloured dresses and lace.

Turn right at the next corner into **Dunlop Street** where, under the **Little India Conservation Project**, there are tiny shops crammed to the ceiling with goods. Unfortunately, these shops are gradually having to make way for sleek facades and spacious salesrooms.

Cut through Clive Street to get to Upper Weld Road. At the next junction turn sharp left into **Cuff Road**, where some smart Indian restaurants are situated. The tables at these restaurants are clean and neatly laid, and most customers eat their food with proper cutlery. Few would object, however, if you ignored your cutlery and used your fingers in the basic but clean and cheap food halls of Serangoon Road. Turn right at the Cuff Road junction.

The ★ **Sri Veeramakaliamman Temple** **50** (6.30am–noon, 5–9pm, Friday and Saturday until 9.30pm) is on the left side of Serangoon Road. Few people will notice the plain external walls, although they may spot the colourful entrance tower; what attracts the Hindu faithful here is the ornate, black statue dedicated to Kali, Shiva's consort.

Diagonally opposite is **Veeraswamy Road**. Even on Sunday, when the majority of shops are closed, the streets here in the heart of Little India are always alive. Groups of Indian migrant workers stand around on street corners. Many gather to meet friends, have a meal or just chat. For these people, it is a brief respite from their jobs as workers in construction sites.

Ahead lies a longish walk. Follow **Kampung Kapor Road** (one of the side roads used to be a famous 'red light' area), **Rowell Road** and **Jalan Besar** as far as the **Lee Ah Leng Trading Company 51** (No 267), a ramshackle bird centre. From inside their beautiful, hand-made bamboo or wire cages, the birds try to outdo each other with their singing. However, this is not a place for the animal rights activist.

Look out for the delightful, old dwellings in Chinese baroque style along ★ **Petain Road**. Colourful tiles with flower decorations brighten up the green facades, making an attractive subject for photographers.

Return to Serangoon Road and cross the road. Thanks to the generosity of a prosperous Indian entrepreneur, the ★ **Sri Srinivasa Perumal Temple 52** (6.30am–noon, 5–9pm, Friday and Saturday until 9.30pm) was fully restored in the 1960s.

Where **Beatty Road** joins **Racecourse Road**, it is the Buddhist gods for a change who attract the crowds. The ★ **Leong San See Temple 53** is an impressive sight with golden dragons crouching on ochre roof tiles. The hubbub inside the temple contrasts with the silent reverence of Hindu temples. The large space at the back is dedicated to the dead. It is interesting to watch the relatives making offerings of food to their ancestors. In accordance with the notice, fish and meat may not be placed on the sacrificial table. The stench of food rotting in the sweltering heat would put even the most stoical Chinese off his prayers.

On the other side of the road, the famous ★ **Temple of 1,000 Lights 54** (daily 7.30am–3.45pm), officially known as the Sakaya Muni Buddha Gaya Temple, outshines all other Buddhist temples. Worshippers may illuminate the seated Buddha for a contribution of S$5. No one is allowed to touch the statue, but there is more to it than meets the eye. Beneath the Buddha is the entrance to a kind of grotto, in which the dying Buddha is portrayed. This temple represents the life's work of a Thai monk who died in 1976. Vutthisasara, as he was known, also provided the temple with a piece of bark – apparently from the tree where Buddha was sitting when he found enlightenment – and this precious relic is now worshipped.

Colourful clothing

41

Leong San See Temple

Temple of 1,000 Lights

A place to meet the people

Route 5

★★ Arab Street

The district by the Rochor River was called Kampung Glam even at the time of the Sultan of Johor. It was to here that the Malayan ruler withdrew when he ceded Singapore to the British. The Malays that lived here then and the immigrants who arrived later from the Middle East, Pakistan, India and the Indonesian islands had one thing in common: they were all Moslems. That is why a purely Islamic quarter grew up very early on and it was named after the main street, Arab Street. The pavements are still the scenes of lively business activity, just like the bazaars, and the faithful are still called to prayer by the muezzins. Remember that haggling over prices is the norm in these parts too. This tour is less about seeing the sights, more about seeing the people: it is a glimpse into the lives of the Singaporean Moslems. During Ramadan, the streets remain quiet until sunset (*see Culture*). Allow a good three hours for this walk, but bargain-hunters will need to set aside more time. Doing deals in the Moslem quarter can take a long time.

Take the underground to Bugis Street and then head south-east along Rochor Road as far as **Beach Road**. This used to be the coast road until the land reclamation project began. Here too, a whole series of narrow shophouses remain and as yet no restoration plans have been implemented. For many years, the merciless tropical climate has been taking its toll on the stone walls which are now beginning to crumble badly. Between roof tiles and in cracks in the wall, where it would seem nothing could grow, vegetation has taken root. And yet, despite the structural decay, commercial activity continues on the ground floor, while families live on the upper floor. Take a walk down the narrow alleys which branch off to the left and see the washing hanging out to dry from the windows. There is a smell of slightly burnt rice, aromatic herbs, of rubbish and mildew.

Arab Street – full to overflowing

    ★★ Arab Street really does do justice to the legendary enterprise of the Arabs. Traders selling basketware, leather goods and brass, batik materials and traditional Moslem clothing jostle beneath the shaded arcades. Many shops simply cannot cope with so many goods, but thankfully there is the 'five foot way', the five-foot wide pavement beneath the arcade which can be stacked high with wares, regardless of whether there is room for the passers-by. It is easy to become entangled in a stand of leather bags or ensnared by a display of batik shawls. Have a good wander round and then order a tea in one of the cafés, but all the other customers will probably be male. In accordance with Islamic tradition, most women who go out on to the streets cover their heads and some also wear a veil over their nose and mouth.

Now turn right twice, first into **Victoria Street** and then into the narrow **Jalan Pinang** alley from where the golden dome of the Sultan Mosque is visible, but it has to be approached from the other side. Turn left into **North Bridge Road**, another lively shopping street where it is not difficult to find unusual souvenirs.

Explore deeper into the strange world of the bazaar by making a short zigzag. Turn left into **Jalan Pisang,** right into **Victoria Street** and then right again into **Jalan Kledek**. Take a look in one of the simple restaurants and watch the *roti prata* show. A few acrobatic movements and the lumps of dough are transformed into wafer-thin pancakes. These are then baked on the hot plate and eaten with sugar or curry. Delicious!

Cross North Bridge Road and proceed a short way along **Kandahar Street**. Turn right into **Muscat Street** and ahead stands the **Sultan Mosque ⑮** (Friday 9–11.30am, 2.30–4pm, otherwise 9am–1pm, 2–4pm). The striking domed roof with its distinctive Arabic features forms part of the biggest mosque in Singapore. It is also the centre of the Islamic faith in the city. Remember that there are strict rules governing entry into a mosque. Filming and taking photographs is not allowed. Women visitors who do not completely cover their arms and legs will be given a long cloak at the entrance. While the men kneel on the carpeted floor to pray, the women must stay in the gallery.

Leave the mosque district via ★ **Bussorah Mall**, once a dilapidated lane, but now a smart, traffic-calmed avenue with palm trees and attractively-restored houses. This is the historic heart of the old Kampung Glam district and, in 1989, parts of it were classified as a conservation area.

The fine two-storey shophouses in **Baghdad Street** (2–10) stand on a very small surface area. Looking rather neglected, in an untidy cul-de-sac called **Sultan Gate**, stands the **Sultan's Palace ⑯**, a building of historical significance in this quarter. Built as a simple palace by the Sultan of Johor in 1867, it still belongs to his descendants and is not open to the public.

Return to North Bridge Street via Baghdad Street and Kandahar Street. Turn left and sniff the air for the delicate blends of perfume at **Jamal Kazura Aromatics** (No 728). At the junction of North Bridge Road and Arab Street, a difficult choice lies in store: selecting one of the numerous, excellent Moslem restaurants with their strongly-spiced, but always pork-free dishes.

And then there is another decision to make: whether to take a taxi or to walk to the Bugis MRT station.

Sultan Mosque

43

Delicate blends at Jamal Kazura

Sentosa Ferry Terminal

Entrance to Sentosa Island

Route 6

★★ Sentosa, Singapore's playground

Only 250m (275 yds) or so from Singapore's main island, the emphasis is on leisure and fun. Sentosa Island used to be a burial place for victims of the local pirates (when it was called Blakang Mati – Back of the Dead) and then served as a fortress for the British.

However, in the 1970s the Singaporean government renamed the island and unashamedly transformed it into a pleasure park. Nothing is left to chance here. The organisation and infrastructure on the island are magnificent. As masses of visitors arrive every weekend, careful crowd management is required. If possible avoid the weekend, but do allow a full day and remember to take a swimming costume. All the main attractions can be reached on buses or via the monorail. The following route has been planned in such a way that the highlights will all have been visited without backtracking.

The ★ **World Trade Centre** at the water's edge on the main island is the starting point for this route (*see page 88*). As well as some attractive shops and restaurants, it boasts the **Guinness World of Records Exhibition** (daily 10am–9pm). Visitors can marvel at the replicas of the tallest man, the smallest woman (59cm/23 inches) and other strange phenomena. The **Maritime Showcase** (Tuesday to Friday 10.30am–6.30pm, Saturday and Sunday 10.30am–8.30pm) contains a model of the harbour.

A basic admission ticket gives you access to the island, its park areas and the beaches plus unlimited rides on the public bus and monorail. Most of the other attractions have their own admission charges. The first attractions on Sentosa can easily be reached on foot from the **Ferry Terminal**. Turn to the left and follow the directions on the board to the **Sentosa Food Centre** ⑤⑦. Here, over a dozen spotlessly clean hawker stalls provide practically every available cuisine in Singapore. This is the ideal place for a second breakfast or an early lunch.

★★ **Fantasy Island** ⑤⑧ (daily 9.30am–7pm), directly behind the food centre, is probably the biggest draw on Sentosa. It is a gigantic waterpark with something for everyone, young or old. The flumes, white-water rapids, eight-track slide and other watery entertainments are surrounded by walls modelled on an ancient Maya settlement. There are also restaurants and snack shops when you get hungry but a word of caution: never go down a slide on a full stomach.

A white-knuckle experience of a different kind is on offer in ★ **Cinemania** (daily 9.30am–8.30pm), just to the right of Fantasy Island. Sit down, get strapped in and enjoy a roller-coaster ride or a journey through an abandoned gold mine, all from a seat in the cinema. Not for those of a feeble disposition.

Orchid Fantasy ⑤⑨ is for the gardener and amateur botanist, who will be interested in the countless varieties of orchids arranged around a pond.

The ★ **Fountain Gardens** ⑥⓪, which extend as far as the ferry terminal, are not quite as colourful. Laid out in

Fantasy Island

45

ROUTE 6

━━━ 1 ━━━ Monorail with station

0   500 m

Musical Fountain

Images of Singapore's history

46

a symmetrical pattern with fountains and over 100 different plant species, they are modelled on the gardens of European stately homes.

The glorious **Musical Fountain** comes to life every evening. This fabulous water and light show is accompanied by classical music played through loudspeakers (Monday to Friday every half hour 7.30–9pm, Saturday at 9.30pm). There are also performances in daylight, but these are not so impressive (10.30am and every half hour 4–5.30pm). You may want to come back to the fountain at the end of your tour of Sentosa as the ferry terminal is only a few minutes' walk away. Watching the water dance to music is a perfect conclusion to a day on Sentosa.

Children will probably prefer **Volcano Land 61** (daily 9am–9pm). This attraction features an ingenious rendering of a volcanic eruption in the labyrinth of a man-made mountain. The 35-m (115-ft) high **Merlion 62** offers a good panoramic view over Sentosa and beyond.

Next, make the climb up the hillside to the informative and extremely interesting history lesson in the exhibition halls of the ★★ **Pioneers of Singapore/ Surrender Chambers/ Festival of Singapore 63** (daily 9am–9pm). In these three exhibitions, life-sized figures tell the story of Singapore's early history, the wars, the road to independence and the harmony in which the different ethnic groups live. Nowhere else is the history of Singapore presented in such an entertaining way.

In the Pioneers exhibition, you will see the conditions in which Chinese coolies were obliged to live – sometimes sharing with Indian convicts – and Mad Ridley and his rubber tree. You will also see Miss Joaquim and her orchid that became Singapore's national flower.

The Surrender Chambers show the ebb and flow of events seen by Singapore in World War II. The British surrender to the Japanese; the Japanese occupy Singapore; the Japanese surrender to the Allies. The exhibition reveals how the more fortunate Singaporeans survived Japan's racial-purity purge.

Now take a stroll through to the **Butterfly Park & Insect Kingdom 64** (Monday to Saturday 9am–6pm, Sunday 9am–6.30pm), where more than 2,000 brightly coloured butterflies flit from flower to flower in a large enclosed garden. There is also a collection of preserved insects – over 4,000 – that includes the world's largest and rarest species.

Cable cars (daily 8.30am–9pm) leave from **Cable Car Plaza** to Mount Faber (on the main island) and back. The ★★ **trip** affords some spectacular views of rusty freighters, gleaming white liners and the busiest container port in the world. Unfortunately, unless a lens filter is fitted, the reflecting cable car windows will spoil any photographs.

Climb out of the cable car, jump on to the monorail and travel from Station 4 to Station 5 (Beruk Station) and **Central Beach** ⑥⑤. This lagoon with its man-made beach of reddish sand is very popular with bathers, despite all the shipping traffic just offshore. Tents may be hired at Sentosa's only camp-site which is situated close by.

Underwater World

Central Beach

Further on, the Monorail Station 6 is within walking distance of the Youth Hostel and also the luxurious **Beaufort Singapore Hotel** (*see page 95*) a little higher up. It has an attractive swimming pool and non-residents are welcome to stop off for a poolside drink.

Station 2 on the monorail is the starting point for the **Nature Walk/ Dragon Trail** through shady jungle vegetation and ★ **Underwater World** ⑥⑥ (daily 9am–9pm), Asia's biggest aquarium where countless tropical fish are kept in a huge tank. What makes Underwater World even more special, however, is the 100-m (110-yd) acrylic tunnel through the middle. Stand on the conveyor belt and watch the fish swimming around.

By the sea, but a longish walk away, the **Shangri-La Rasa Sentosa Resort** is another luxury hotel with recreational facilities and a crèche for younger guests.

Show of culture in the Asian Village

In the underground passages of the old **Fort Siloso** ⑥⑦ (Station 3; daily 9am–7pm), exhibits and displays retell the ironic story of the battle for Singapore during World War II. The British were convinced Siloso's big guns would protect Singapore. Unfortunately, the guns pointed out to sea and the Japanese came through the jungle on bicycles with flat tyres. In the following siege, the British surrendered a few days before the Japanese planned to withdraw because of lack of supplies.

Take the monorail back to the ferry terminal, perhaps stopping at the **Asian Village** on the way to sample some food, buy souvenirs or watch a street performance by one of the various cultural troupes.

Route 7

★ Jurong

The drained marshland to the west of Singapore has turned into one of the most important industrial locations on the island. Proximity to the container port was one factor in its development, but the existence of a good road network and the underground railway also played a part. 'Industrial parks' have been added and the flower beds and green spaces give some justification to this name. Between the docks and the city centre, spacious parkland provides rest and relaxation and, at the weekend, many city dwellers are attracted by the wildlife parks. The sights described here are not all within easy reach of each other and so do not easily lend themselves to a self-contained tour. It would also not be possible to cover them all in one day. The best way to get from one to the other is via the excellent public transport network.

Chinese Garden

Not surprisingly, the ★ **Chinese Garden** ❻❽ on Yuan Ching Road (Monday to Saturday 9am–7pm, Sunday 8.30am–7pm; nearest MRT station: Chinese Garden) is a favourite spot for happy couples to pose for their wedding photographs. Colourful pavilions and towers, delightful arched bridges and ponds dotted with sea roses and water lilies all make an idyllic backdrop. Everything is set in a meticulously tended 13-hectare (32-acre) Song-style garden, surrounded by the waters of the Jurong Lake. It is the perfect place to take a leisurely stroll, to ride in a pedalo or to inhale the aromatic scents of the herb garden.

Japanese Garden

Next to the Chinese garden and accessible via a bridge, is the **Japanese Garden** ❻❾, also within the Jurong Lake (Monday to Saturday 9am–7pm, Sunday 8.30am–7pm). About the same size as its Chinese counterpart, the garden displays the main features of Japanese landscaping, such as a concern for detail, clear lines and simple forms. Although the shrubs in the stone garden, alongside the running water and waterfalls have been positioned with considerable care, the impression is one of random planting. To fully appreciate the oriental gardens, allow 2½ hours for each.

For those unschooled in ancient Chinese history, the ★ **Tang Dynasty Village** on Yuan Ching Road ❼❶ (daily 9.30am–6.30pm; nearest MRT station: Lakeside; bus Nos 154/240) is an entertaining way of discovering a little about life in China during the first millennium. Just as in the Middle Kingdom's old capital, Chang'an (modern Xian) some 2,000 years ago, there is a tea-house, a temple, pagodas and a **Chamber of a Thousand Pleasures** (for

ROUTE 7 2 km
0

Pan Island Expressway

Lakeside | Chinese Garden

JURONG WEST NEW TOWN

JURONG/EAST NEW TOWN

Jurong East

Ayer Rajah

West Coast Highway

Clementi

Pandan Res.

Damar Laut | Selat Jurong

viewing only!). Enter the Ghost Mansion and suffer at the hands of old Chinese spirits. Get to know the names and faces of the Chinese emperors at the **Waxworks Museum**. Enjoy a meal at the **Tai He Lou Theatre Restaurant**, while a troupe of acrobats provides the entertainment (daily 1.15pm, 7.30pm; meals start an hour before). To make the most of this historical theme park – which is still expanding – allow three hours.

Tang Dynasty troupers

The ★ **Singapore Science Centre/Omni Theatre** 🐬 on Science Centre Road (Tuesday to Sunday, 10am–6pm; nearest MRT station is Jurong East, then on foot or by bus No 335) will enthrall children and technophiles for hours. All the secrets of science and technology are revealed. In a special 'hands-on' gallery, activities include a simulated flight landing. In the **Omni Theatre** a series of films is shown on a huge, hemispheric screen. Planetarium shows take place every hour 10am–9pm (except 1pm and 5pm). There is easily enough at the complex to keep visitors occupied for two hours.

★★ **Jurong Bird Park** 🐬 on Jalan Ahmad Ibrahim (daily 9am–6pm; nearest MRT station is Boon Lay and then by bus Nos 251/253/255) boasts over 3,500 birds and 400 species. Some 1,200 birds fly around in the biggest walk-in aviary in the world. Some 2 hectare (5 acres) of land are enclosed by a huge net. If **Breakfast with the Birds** (daily 9–11am) is too early, then watch one of the shows, such as the **JBP All Star Birdshow** when the flamingos dance to a Caribbean rhythm (daily 11am and 3pm). Another favourite with the crowds is the **Kings of the Skies Show** (daily 4pm) when eagles and falcons demonstrate their skills. To make the most of the Bird Park, allow a good 2½ hours, even with the monorail and bus.

Bird Park residents

49

At the **Jurong Crocodile Paradise** 🐬 next door, the fearsome reptiles look well fed, but then they do receive two generous feeds each day (10.15am and 5pm). In addition, they are expected to engage each other in battle (11.45am and 2pm, Sundays also at 4pm) and then there is the **Dundee Show** at 10.45am and 3pm. An **Underwater Viewing Gallery** enables visitors to watch the crocodiles from below, while children particularly enjoy visiting the special enclosure where the delicate baby crocs are kept. A tour takes about 90 minutes.

Magnificent Chinese porcelain in Ming dynasty style is produced and sold at the ★★ **Ming Village** 🐬 at 32 Pandan Road (daily 9am–6pm; nearest MRT station: Clementi, then bus No 78). Visitors can see freshly-thrown clay turn into an elegant, classical-style, hand-painted object of beauty. A metre-high (3-ft) vase with the characteristic blue motifs costs in the region of S$8,000. The staff will be happy to wrap and despatch home any fragile items. To send a large vase will cost about S$330.

Ming Village porcelain

Unmistakably Malay

Shade of colour

Route 8

The Malay and Peranakan quarters

The Malays have clearly stayed in control in Geylang Serai. On the streets, the women and girls wear colourful costumes and cover their hair with Islamic-style cloths or hoods. Many of the men wrap the traditional *sarungs* around their hips. In the lively Malay markets the national traditions are still very much in evidence. Appetising aromas waft from the many small snack bars and simple restaurants and it is hard to resist sampling some of the delicious Malay specialities.

There are treats for the taste buds too in the Katong quarter where clear traces of the Peranakans (*see page 9*), the descendants of the Straits-born Chinese remain. The ageing shopping streets are lined by splendid old buildings, many of which are undergoing restoration. Nearby, wealthy Singaporeans live in detached houses, while the middle classes occupy rather plain residental blocks.

This tour involves a lot of walking, but to compensate there will be plenty of opportunities for breaks. Allow about four hours, preferably in the morning, when the streets are at their busiest.

The ideal starting point in Geylang Serai is the **Paya Lebar** MRT station. The ★★ **Malay Village** ⓲ (daily 10am–10pm is only a short distance away). The aim of this complex is to illustrate the history, culture and lifestyle of the Malays. Souvenir shops and restaurants serving Malay specialities occupy the traditional wooden houses with their pointed gables.

Displays in a small **Cultural Museum** shed light on the Malay heritage. The basic wooden huts in the **Kampung Nostalgia** take visitors back to the Geylang Serai of the

1950s and a magnificent wedding celebration is enacted with the aid of puppets. Romantics will not want to miss **Lagenda Fantasi** (daily between noon and 9pm as required). Ali Baba and other oriental legends are enchantingly retold using multivision effects.

On the other side of Geylang Serai lies the ★★ **Geylang Serai Market** 76 (daily, early in the morning until dusk, during Ramadan until late into the night). *Serai* is the Malay word for lemon grass, a crop that used to be cultivated here. The spice continues to be an important ingredient in Malay cooking. Also gone forever are the many little mills that converted the grass to citronella cooking oil.

Geylang Serai Market

The market is a maze of tightly-packed stalls, many of which sag under the weight of fabrics, household goods, jewellery and artificial flowers. In the adjoining food market, various aromas waft through the air, enticing shoppers into snack bars. Despite the crowds, nobody pushes or shoves as the shoppers shuffle past the mountains of goods.

Return to Geylang Serai and cross Changi Road. On the left-hand side, the busy **Joo Chiat Complex** shopping centre boasts a wide range of typically Malay goods, but it is not as interesting as the Geylang Serai market.

51

Many businesses along **Joo Chiat Road** are run from the ground floor of stone shophouses, which have long outlasted the old Malay structures made from wood. Many traditional professions survive here in the same way as the Chinese cottage industries (*see page 15*). At **Kway Guan Huat** (No 95) spring rolls are still made by hand in the morning and then sold throughout the day. A workshop diagonally opposite produces hand-made rattan furniture, which is then displayed on the pavement.

About 700m (750yds) further on, make a brief detour to the left into ★ **Koon Seng Road** to discover the grand Peranakan houses. Their facades, richly decorated with colourful tiles, testify to the wealth of the original owners. They also indicate that this is the right route to **Katong**. Take a close look at the shape of the air-vents above the windows. What looks like butterflies are, in fact, bats. Like the Chinese, the Peranakans believed that these creatures brought good luck.

Sri Seng Aga Vinayagar Temple

One or two night clubs are situated further along Joo Chiat Road. These do not open until much later when an unambiguous red light glows. There is, however, room for a place of worship: the **Sri Seng Aga Vinayagar Temple 77**. This fine-looking neighbourhood temple was built for the district's small Hindu community. The faithful come here to revere the elephant-headed god of wisdom, Ganesh, whose statue stands above the entrance.

At the end of the road, turn left into **East Coast Road**. The ★ **Katong Bakery & Confectionery** at No 75 (8am–7pm) sells delicious curry puffs and cream cakes, prepared to a traditional Peranakan recipe. For an air-conditioned environment, if the temperature rises, turn right along East Coast Road and make for the **Katong Shopping Centre**. Attractions here include the chance to sample birds' nests (*see Food and Drink, page 72*). Otherwise, head east on the left side of East Coast Road. Some basic *Nonya* restaurants serve *laksa* (rice noodles with fish in a spicy coconut milk gravy).

Katong Bakery & Confectionery

One interesting shop is the **Katong Antique House** (No 208). The owner, Peter Wee, is a descendant of an old Peranakan family and he will be happy to show you his collection of antiques, but it is advisable to make an appointment (tel: 345 8544). Also of interest are the pawn shops. Anything that is not redeemed within six months is put on sale. Occasionally, some delightful jewellery and watches are sold at very reasonable prices. Do not pass the ★ **Daun Pandan Rice Dumpling** (No 226) without trying the triangle bundles of sticky rice stuffed with seasoned meat and wrapped in pandanus leaves.

Either end the tour here – or take a taxi and cool off by the ★ **East Coast Park**. During the daytime, walkers can enjoy miles of paths and cooling sea breezes, while fitness freaks can choose between a number of different sporting facilities. In the evening, it is the food served in the numerous seafood restaurants that draws the visitors.

Seafood draws the visitors

Route 9

The other islands

There are about 60 islands off Singapore's 'mainland'. Few are accessible to tourists and only about half of them are inhabited. Malay fishermen and farmers living in rather primitive villages make up the majority of the population. However, it is on these *pulau*, the Malay word for island, that the other side of Singapore can still be seen.

Unfortunately, tourism is gaining ground on the more attractive islands and luxury hotels, beaches and leisure facilities will, the authorities hope, attract increasing numbers of visitors. A couple of islands are served by regular ferries. The only way to reach the others is to join a tour or hire a boat.

According to legend, ★ **Kusu Island** (Pulau Tembakul) is a giant turtle that became an island to save a Malay and a Chinese sailor from drowning. As a token of their gratitude, the Malay built a holy shrine and the Chinese built a temple.

53

Kusu Island does have two holy sites that support this tale: Moslem pilgrims regularly make the trip to the **Keramat Abdul Rahman**, while, in the ninth month of the Chinese lunar calendar, the **Tua Pekong Temple** is the destination for a spectacular pilgrimage by boat. However, this attractive temple that stands above the water on stilts is worth a visit at any time of the year. Furthermore, there is a fine bathing beach within easy reach.

Kusu Island is 7km (4 miles) from Singapore's main island and no overnight accommodation is available. Boats leave from the World Trade Centre (Monday to Saturday 10am and 1.30pm. The last return ferry is at 3.30pm. On Sunday there are additional ferries between 9am and 7.20pm and the last return ferry is at 8pm).

Lazarus Island (Pulau Sakijang Pelepah) nearby is currently being transformed into a holiday resort. Thanks to a land reclamation project, by the end of the millennium Lazarus will have merged with the neighbouring island of **Pulau Renget** and will then be linked by a footbridge to **St John's Island** (Pulau Sakijang Bendera). Although the beaches could be tidier and the sand finer, the slightly undulating island is very popular with Singaporeans. That is probably because, away from the levelled-off footpaths and quite cheap, self-catering accommodation (bungalows and dormitories), the landscape is unspoilt. Boat tours leave from the World Trade Centre and Kusu Island (see above for ferry times to Kusu Island. Last return ferry, Monday to Saturday 2.45pm, Sunday 8.20pm).

Family dip

Pulau Hantu (southwest of Sentosa) and **Sisters Island** southwest of St John's) are favourite haunts of experienced divers who want to explore the clear waters and observe the abundant fish. Beware of the powerful currents off Pulau Hantu. No regular boat service exists, so the beaches and picnic sites here are usually empty. No overnight accommodation is available either and the only way to get to the island is to hire a boat by Clifford Pier or the World Trade Centre.

About 70 Malay families still live on the island of **Pulau Seking**. In their homes in the *kampong*, the traditional wooden houses still sit on stilts over the water; it is as if time has stood still. While many of the younger generation have left to work in the refineries or in the factories by the harbour, the old folk continue to fish, as they always have, in their *jongs* – hand-carved, long, narrow outriggers with bright canvas sails. To walk around the island will take about 30 minutes. Getting to the 4-sq km (1½-sq mile) rocky outcrop will take about 40 minutes (boats leave from Clifford Pier). The government has plans to 'develop' the island in the near future.

★ **Pulau Ubin** lies in the narrow Johor Strait between Malaysia and Singapore. Malay village life continues amid the luxuriant tropical vegetation, but the population is dwindling rapidly. Some 3,000 people once lived on the island, but now only about 400 remain in the simple wooden dwellings.

A 15-minute boat ride from the jetty in **Changi Village** is all it takes to reach Ubin. Ferries operate between 7am and 9pm, but only when 12 passengers are waiting. The island, which is twice as big as Sentosa, is popular with nature lovers who bring their tents and provisions in order to observe the wide variety of wildlife. There is no accommodation on the island and only one restaurant (in the village).

Visitors wishing to explore the island on the unmade tracks should allow a full day. Mountain bikes, plus a simple map of the island, can be hired in the village (Yen Fa Bicycle Rental, daily 8am–5pm, S$3 per day). Taxis are also available (about S$20 per hour), but the drivers do not speak English. The best way to overcome this problem is to buy a map of the island at the cycle hire centre and then show the taxi driver the two sights that are essential viewing: the colourful **Thai Temple**, which was built by Thai monks, and the **Ma Chor Temple**, a magnificent Chinese temple by the seashore, from where Singapore's impressive skyline is visible.

Limestone is quarried in certain parts of the island and 'Blasting Areas' are indicated.

Pulau Ubin from Changi beach

Old quarry on the island

Further Sights

Alkaff Mansion

There are not that many tourist sights away from the main routes already described. Most of them can be reached easily as public transport is good. If necessary, take a taxi. At weekends and holidays, Singapore families head out of town to the gardens, leisure parks and the zoo, so, if possible, try to choose a weekday.

55

★ **Chettiar's Hindu Temple** at 15 Tank Road, west of Fort Canning Hill (daily 8am–noon and 5.30pm–8.30pm; nearest MRT station: Dhoby Ghaut then on foot via Clemenceau Avenue, *see map on page 21*) is the popular name for the splendid **Sri Thandayuthapani Temple**, which was completed in 1983 with funds from the wealthy Chettiar community. One particularly impressive feature is the roof which is fitted with 48 windows that catch the rays of the rising and the setting sun. Crowds of devout Hindus fill the temple during the Hindu festivals, notably Thaipusam (*see page 67*).

The ★ **Alkaff Mansion** at 10 Telok Blangah Green on Mount Faber (best reached by taxi) was built in the 1920s by a wealthy Arab family by the name of Alkaff. Sumptuous gatherings were held at this magnificent mansion with its superb view of the coast and Sentosa Island. Lavish restoration work during the 1990s returned the splendour to the thick stone walls without destroying the nostalgic atmosphere. Guests at this opulent restaurant can choose from the **Mansion Hall** (oriental/western cuisine), the **Dining Room** *(rijstaffel)* and the **West Terrace** (seafood barbecue), but the speciality is definitely the colonial Dutch-Indonesian *rijstaffel*. Before dinner, enjoy a drink and watch the sun set in the **Verandah Bar**. Table reservations are recommended.

The mansion's dining room

Haw Par Villa

★★ **Haw Par Villa** at 262 Pasir Panjang Road (daily 9am–6pm; nearest MRT station: Clementi (W8), then SBS bus No 10) is a high-tech Chinese mythological theme park. Every conceivable god, hero, beauty, demon and mythical beast from the world of myth and legend is assembled here – much to the delight of the locals.

One of the main attractions is the 2,000-seater South China Sea amphitheatre, where audiences receive an introduction to Chinese opera (*see page 65*). Three hours here is barely enough to unravel the sometimes complicated tales that make up Chinese mythology. You can be helped, however, by the storyteller **Hoy Hay** in the **Legends and Heroes Theatre** (every 30 minutes from 9.30am), and children will be fascinated by the colourful, electronically-controlled puppets.

The villa was funded by the two 'Tiger Balm' brothers, Aw Boon Haw and Aw Boon Par, who made their fortune from Tiger Balm, the aromatic ointment that is used the world over to treat headaches and minor ailments.

Botanical Gardens

The ★ **Botanical Gardens** is a huge, green oasis in the middle of the city, not far from Orchard Road. Opened in 1859, the site is currently being transformed into an internationally-regarded Botanical Garden. The government is investing some S$50 million into the project. Not only is the garden being enlarged to 52 hectares (128 acres), but other changes include improvements to the infrastructure, guided walks and, at the entrance in Cluny Road, a modern Visitor Centre with audio-visual aids. The Singaporean government insists on perfection, so existing areas, such as the orchid gardens and herb and spice beds, will also be smartened up.

The grand re-opening of the Botanical Gardens is due to take place at the beginning of 1997.

The ★ **Bukit Timah Nature Reserve** (nearest MRT station: Newton Station (N4), then bus No 67,170 or 171 or TIBS bus No 182) is, for the most part, unspoilt jungle at the heart of the island, just 12km (7 miles) from the city centre. Visitors can explore this wildlife reserve on well-marked footpaths and a brochure showing the possible circular tours is available at the entrance. At 165m (540ft), **Bukit Timah Hill** is the highest point on the island and it is worth making the climb to view Seletar reservoir. Allow a few hours, even half a day, to do justice to this fascinating reserve, but do not forget to apply plenty of mosquito repellent. While the pestilential insects have been driven out of the city, walkers will be mercilessly attacked unless they are well protected. The Visitor Centre is on Hindhede Drive, tel: 470 9900.

Jungle warriors, Bukit Timah

The **Zoological Garden** on Mandai Lake Road (daily 8.30am–6pm; nearest MRT station: Ang Mo Kio (N9), then SBS bus No 138) houses over 2,000 animals. Most of them are kept, not in cages or behind wire, but in spacious, humane enclosures surrounded by ditches. Sometimes called the 'open zoo', it is noted for its work in breeding orangutans – visitors are, therefore, cordially invited to 'Breakfast or High Tea with the Orang Utan' (daily 9am or 4pm). After breakfast, the next highlight of the day is a photocall with the apes and a glass of orange juice. The 30-minute Animal Shows in the amphitheatre are also worth watching (daily 10.30am, 11.30am, 2.30pm, 3.30pm), while the Polar Bear Show takes place every day at 10.05am, 1.05pm and 4.45pm. Elephant and camel rides are also available. Without making any longer stops, a full tour of the zoo can be completed in about 45 minutes on the shuttle bus. But why hurry?

Feeding time

The ★★ **Night Safari Park** on Mandai Lake Road near the zoo (daily 7.30pm–midnight, nearest MRT station: Ang Mo Kio (N9), then SBS bus No 138) is open during the hours of darkness, so that animal lovers can observe nocturnal animals such as rhinoceros, elephants, tigers and crocodiles. Altogether, 1,200 animals are kept in 47 different habitats within the park. A 45-minute tour by train passes seemingly open and discreetly lit enclosures. Flash photography is forbidden. There are also three walking tours which together take about two hours (2.8km/1¾ miles). No one need be worried about going astray in the dark or treading on a lion's tail. Staff posted at regular intervals make sure everyone is on the right route. Evening meals are available in the adjoining restaurant either from an *à la carte* menu or a very reasonably priced buffet. To see the animals at their most active, try to get round before 9.30pm; the last tour starts at 11.15pm.

The ★ **Mandai Orchid Gardens**, a 15-minute walk from the zoo on Mandai Lake Road (daily 8.30am–5.30pm; nearest MRT station: Ang Mo Kio (N9), then SBS bus No 138) boast over 300 species of orchids. They grow in a mixture of charcoal and brick and some clamber up poles while others hang in sprays from pots. This is one of the world's finest orchid displays.

Lovers of these marvellous plants can enjoy the colourful blooms in the gardens throughout the whole year – and, if they wish, even take them home. The 'Orchid Gift Box Service' will deliver the elegant flowers to any address in the world.

58

Birds at Seng Poh

Birds are greatly admired by the Chinese and they are a common sight in many Singaporean flats. Owners frequently spend hours teaching their beloved pets to sing, sometimes with the aid of cassettes – a well-trained bird can be worth several thousand dollars.

Bird lovers congregate with their birds every Sunday morning at about 10am in the **Seng Poh Coffee Shop** (corner of Tiong Bahru and Seng Poh Road; nearest MRT station: Tiong Bahru). Undisturbed by the traffic noise, the birds give of their best. The cages are not placed close together by accident or through lack of space – this is how beginners learn from their more advanced friends. Visitors to the café are, of course, able to enjoy the avian concert over a cup of coffee.

★★ **Singapore Harbour** handles almost half a million tonnes of cargo every year – and that is a world record. There are two ways tourists can view the vast harbour area – from the water or the air.

Singapore's Clifford Pier

A boat trip around the harbour takes tourists past tiny offshore islands and many more or less seaworthy vessels that lie at anchor further out to sea. The cost of a lunch or an evening meal is included in the price.

Perhaps the most romantic way is to make the trip in a Chinese junk, such as the *Fairwind* (from Clifford Pier, Eastwind Organisation, tel: 533 3432; daily at 10.30am, 3pm, 4pm and 6pm).

Some may prefer a disco on the air-conditioned catamaran *Equator Dream* (from Clifford Pier, J&N Cruises, tel: 533 2733; daily at 10pm).

The three-hour 'Port Discovery Tour' run by Sentosa Discovery Tours (tel: 277 9654; Tuesday to Sunday at 2.30pm) takes tourists behind the scenes in the computer-operated port.

If you get seasick, perhaps you should take to the air over the harbour on the cable car that links Mount Faber with Sentosa island via the World Trade Centre on the harbour edge (*see pages 46 and 88*).

Changi is the name of the ultra-modern airport and the nearby plain, prefabricated village. The coastal strip around the landing stage for the ferry to Pulau Ubin (*see Route 9, page 54*) and the marina where wealthy Singaporeans moor their boats are much more attractive areas.

Changi is also the site of Singapore's biggest prison and **Changi Prison Chapel and Museum**, a memorial to the prisoner-of-war camp run by the Japanese during World War II (Monday to Saturday 9.30am–12.30pm, 2–4.30pm; nearest MRT station: Tanah Merah (E9), then SBS bus No 2). Its focal point is the replica of a small wooden chapel hand-built by the allied soldiers as a symbol of hope. Photographs, documents and everyday objects exhibited in the nearby museum give some impression of the cruelty that the prisoners had to endure. James Clavell's famous novel *King Rat* (1962) powerfully describes the suffering of the prisoners-of-war in Changi.

The Chapel at Changi

Mangrove swamp takes up almost a third of the 17-hectare (42-acre) **Pasir Ris Park** on the northeast coast of Singapore (Nearest MRT station: Pasir Ris (E12), then SBS bus No 21 or 350). The birds and the marshy primeval forest that once covered a large part of Singapore can be seen from wooden staging. Pasir Ris is also Singapore's showpiece residential quarter.

Do not miss the ★ **Siong Lim Temple** at 184 E Jalan Toa Payoh (daily 9am–5pm; nearest MRT station: Toa Payoh (N6)). Built in 1908, this impressive temple complex with its sweeping, green tiled roofs is situated amid new development by the Expressway. Everywhere between the bright red walls, incense sticks and oil lamps burn in honour of Buddha. It is one of the biggest and, in the afternoon, one of the liveliest temples in Singapore.

Siong Lim Temple

Excursions

Malaysia and Indonesia are very close to Singapore so it is easy to make the short crossing, with organised tours or independently. To enter either country you need a passport valid for another six months. Malaysia allows you to stay two months without a visa, Indonesia three months. Anti-malaria inoculations are recommended. The destinations below are for travellers with limited time. For all excursions, you can be back in Singapore within two days.

Causeway to Johor Bahru
Abu Bakar Mosque

Johor Bahru

This Malaysian town lies on the other side of the Causeway, about half an hour's drive away from the centre of Singapore. Fuel tanks have to be at least three-quarters full when vehicles leave Singapore, and the authorities check gauges to stop locals driving into Malaysia to buy cheap fuel. In Johor Bahru it soon becomes apparent that practically everything is cheaper in Malaysia, particularly textiles and arts and crafts.

Look for the **Istana Besar** (Sultan's Palace) in its beautiful garden, the **Abu Bakar Mosque** above the town and the **cemetery** which contains the splendid tombs of Johor's royal family.

Most Singapore taxis are not licensed for Malaysia, but plenty of buses journey between Singapore and Johor Bahru (express bus from Ban San Street/Rochor Canal Road or the slower SBS No 170 from Queen Street). Organised bus tours take about three and a half hours. RMG Tours, tel: 337 3377. Buses leave at 9.30am every day.

Kukup

Most of the wooden houses in this old fishing village on the southwest coast of Malaysia stand on stilts, but most visitors are attracted by the freshly-caught fish served up in the restaurants. However, Kukup is about 100km (60 miles) away and it is not easy to reach by scheduled bus service. A more convenient way to travel is by organised bus tour (about nine hours). Visits to a fish farm and a rubber plantation are also usually included in the tour. Holiday Tours, tel: 738 2622. Buses leave at 9am every day.

Desaru

The 20-km (12-mile) sandy beach on the southeast coast of Malaysia is a favourite haunt for Singaporeans wanting to re-charge themselves. There is always plenty going on in the hotels at weekends and during the holidays. A hire car is the ideal way of getting there, but organised bus tours are available. These take two days and the fare includes overnight accommodation. Gray Line Tours, tel: 331 8244. Buses leave at 9am every day.

Malacca

Malacca, on Malaysia's west coast almost 220km (135 miles) from Singapore, is a town with a long history. Until the 16th century, the town was ruled by a powerful sultan and his family, but they were deposed by the Portuguese. The Dutch followed and then the British.

Several buildings reflect a European influence. The **Stadthuys**, for example, was built in the mid 17th century

Part of the colonial heritage

by the Dutch. It now houses the **Historical Museum**, which documents the town's colonial heritage. In 1741, the Dutch also built the nearby **Christ Church**, which retains much of its original seating. On the hill to the rear stands the ruined **St Paul's Church**. This dates from 1521, when the Portuguese were in control. It is worth making the climb to the top if only for the view over the Straits of Malacca. A now empty grave once contained the body of Francisco Xavier who worked as a missionary in the town. His remains were later taken to India. The path down the other side of the hill leads to **Porta de Santiago**, a huge stone gateway that is all that remains from the Portuguese fortress known as 'A Famosa' (1511). The **Cheng Hoon Teng Temple**, Malaysia's oldest Buddhist temple (1645) stands on the other side of the Melaka River.

61

Cheng Hoon Temple detail

There are tours to Malacca from Singapore, but the journey time prevents travellers doing justice to all the sights or having a good wander round the excellent antique shops (e.g. Jl. Hang Jebat). Sightseeing Tour East, 3C River Valley Road, Clarke Quay (#01-24/25 Cannery Block), tel: 332 3755. It is worth staying for two or three days if time permits. The commendable **Malacca Village Park Plaza Resort** ($$$) is about 10 minutes' drive from Malacca in a peaceful spot by a lake. Tel: 06/323600, fax: 325955.

Batam Island

The ferry to this Indonesian island takes around 30 minutes. Ferries leave from the World Trade Centre every half-hour 8am–7pm. Tourism has brought rapid changes to this island. Hotels have been built and new roads laid to villages that were recently only accessible by boat. Batam is now a supply base for the offshore oil industry. Yet lush vegetation, peace and unspoilt settlements still remain, and many Singaporeans come here for rest and relaxation. Only the beaches leave something to be desired. The business centre of Nagoya was established by the Japanese during World War II.

Day trips usually include a tour of an oil installation. RMG Tours, tel: 337 3377. Fast boats leave from Finger Pier by the World Trade Centre on Monday, Wednesday and Friday at 9.40am. Late bookings for Indonesia are often available at reduced rates in the World Trade Centre (2nd floor). Sinba Cruise, tel: 270 7779.

Art and Customs

Opposite: Chinese and Hindu Temples side by side

The racial mix of Chinese, Malay and Indian determines the culture of the city state. The most impressive buildings are either the temples belonging to the different faiths or the monumental edifices from the colonial era. Singapore's house facades no longer follow the traditional Asian models, as the planners and architects have sought to give the city a thoroughly modern look. Steel, concrete, glass and chrome have replaced the old houses. Where tourism has kept the old shophouses intact, the lines of streets often look drab and sterile. Instead of a full facelift, old walls have simply been smartened up with new ones. Soon the traditional craftsmen, such as woodcarvers, dyers, potters and goldsmiths, will be driven out of existence as their tiny workshops in houses renovated by the state are becoming too expensive.

So Singaporean culture finds expression less in its old buildings and more in its ancient customs and colourful ethnic festivals.

The Malays

Lighted lanterns at the Mooncake Festival

63

Until recently mixed marriages between Moslems and other faiths were the exception. In accordance with ancient traditions, weddings last three days, an occasion when silk and brocade costumes are paraded. Of more importance than the happy couple is the *mak andam*, the woman who organises the expensive spectacle and exhausting banquet. She will be responsible for the wedding garments (six different costumes for both the bride and bridegroom is not exceptional), the complicated make-up and the correct course of the wedding rituals.

A Malay family name lasts for little more than one generation, as children always add the name of their father to their own. Sometimes the words 'bin' or 'binte' are placed between christian and family names, meaning 'son of' or 'daughter of'.

Modestly-dressed Malays

The natural warmth and hospitality of the Malays is overwhelming. Foreigners should, however, be aware of certain taboos: men should not touch women (and vice versa) and revealing clothing is generally frowned upon. Most Malay women in Singapore do not bother with the veil, but in the Geylang Serai and Kampong Glam quarters, it is common to see women wearing the *tudung*, a cloth that covers hair and neck. Some also wear the *sarung*, a long, traditional skirt that is draped around the hips.

The Indians

Brightly-coloured saris, the fabric interwoven with gold thread stand out in the streets of Little India (*see pages 38–41*), but many women also wear the Punjabi dress of northern India: a knee-length shirt over long trousers. The Indian women's gold jewellery is also impossible to miss. Chains and bracelets are the traditional wedding gifts of Indian husbands and goldsmiths' shop windows are invariably surrounded by young women. Only widows leave their jewellery at home.

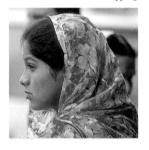

Out shopping

Many marriages are still arranged by parents and a married woman can be identified by the dab of red powder along the centre parting or by a red spot on the forehead, although that can also be an adornment worn by an unmarried woman. Family names are not usual. Usually, the son adds his father's final name to his own or else places the initial letter of his father's name before his own. Women adopt their husband's name upon marriage.

Almost everything is done with the right hand, whether it is eating, handing over a present or simply returning change. The left, 'unclean' hand is used for bodily hygiene. As for relations with the opposite sex, men should keep at least an arm's length from women.

Indian temple detail

Indian temples

No one may enter a Hindu temple wearing shoes. But before going inside the building, take a look at the *gopuram*, the colourful gate tower with statues of the deities – Walt Disney might well have had a hand in their production! These images of gods, piled one on top of the other, are typical of the temples of southern India. Even inside, illustrations and representations of the complex world of Hindu gods abound. Centrally positioned and in a lavishly decorated shrine stands the god to whom the temple is dedicated – and he will be guarded by other statues. Sometimes the sacred section of the temple is partitioned off with bars or curtains.

Devotees will present the statue with sacrificial offerings such as garlands, fresh tumeric or opened coconuts whose white flesh symbolises purity. People are always coming and going. The followers who prostrate themselves on the floor are giving themselves unconditionally to their god. The brahman, as the Hindu priest is called, is the medium between god and his devotees. He has many often complicated rituals to perform, especially during the regular temple festivals.

The Chinese

The Chinese love to show others what they have and what they are. The 'yuppie' sons and daughters of the rich have simple taste – only the best will do. Whether it is clothing, music, theatre, car or flat, for the young Chinese of Singapore it must be western. Even a western christian name is essential. The boy christened Lee Yock Suan (Lee is by far the commonest surname), will probably be referred to as Paul Lee. Only the older generation still live in the traditional two- or three-storey shophouses – that is, shop on the ground floor, living quarters upstairs.

By contrast, *Wayang*, better known to foreigners as Chinese opera, is pure, unadulterated China. This traditional, musical theatre – *wayang* comes from Malay and means 'play' – is performed on simple stages in all parts of Singapore. Its monotonous rhythms and clanging cymbals are not always to westerners' taste, but it is certainly fascinating to watch the actors in their colourful costumes and with their faces made up to signify the age, status, views and morality of the character they are depicting. The simple plots are derived from ancient Chinese legends, myths and history.

Chinese temples

It is easy to gain the impression that a Chinese temple is no different from a market place. Everyone chatters and laughs, families unwrap their food, mothers scold their unruly children who run around the temple corridors. But is there any room for reverence?

There is, despite appearances. It involves the faithful lighting their three incense sticks (symbolising past, present and future) and holding them up in ardent prayer; it involves them sharing a meal with the dead in front of a memorial plaque to their ancestors. Religion is a kind of game that believers play with the countless temple gods. The rules are: 'You give to me and I will give to you'. Offerings are given in return for advice, which the temple guard even writes down. Another popular trade-off involves the statues of the two 'penitent players'. Hanging round their necks are bags containing tips for the forthcoming lottery. Of course, any winners must share their prizes with the tipsters.

Chinese devotee and temple

65

Chinese Opera

Burning money to the monkey God

Lion guard

The Chinese assign a different responsibility to each of their gods and goddesses and so there are many different statues in Chinese temples. Buddha is one of them, but others include the god of war, the Monkey God and the emperor's gods, not forgetting the guards and the spirits from the mythological world. A lion and lioness traditionally protect the entrance, but people have little confidence in their vigilance and erect knee-high barriers as well, to trip up any evil spirits.

Feng shui

Anyone who dreads encountering a black cat will understand about *feng shui*, but the Chinese would be appalled if *feng shui* were to be equated with superstition. For the Chinese, *feng shui* (meaning 'wind and water') is a science, based on the Buddhist concept of *yin* and *yang*, although it is accepted that demons and spirits also play their part. In practice, important events in a person's life, such as marriage, birth of children, the construction of a new house and funerals must be conducted according to certain rules so that harmony with nature is not destroyed. Evil influences and spirits must be warded off. That is why the Chinese build the entrance to their houses away from the street, otherwise the spirits would have easy access to the interior. A mirror attached to the front of the house helps to keep evil spirits away. Even modern housebuilders pay heed to *feng shui*. If a business does not prosper, then something is probably wrong with the *feng shui*. A waterfall by the entrance (which will stop the money flowing away) can sometimes work wonders.

To make absolutely certain that things are right, a geomancy expert may have to be called in. One of the most famous and best-paid geomancy specialists is called Master Tan. He will also know what a child should be called and will be able to predict the child's future according to the Chinese horoscope. His office is open to the public and visitors can find out more about *feng shui* there (Monday to Friday, 10am–7pm). Master Tan, Way Chinese Geomancy Centre, 149 Rochor Road (Fu Lu Shou Complex, near Bugis Street, #02-11), tel: 336 3060.

Literature

In the first half of this century, important western literary figures such as Joseph Conrad, Somerset Maugham and Rudyard Kipling were colourful players in the island's colonial life, and their accounts– often centred on the Raffles Hotel *(see pages 26 and 77)* – provide an insight into the way wealthy British settlers lived in Singapore. The more down-to-earth writings of modern Singaporean authors such as Tan Kok Seng and Catherine Lim deal with the day-to-day problems of life in the growing city state.

Festivals

No other country in the world can offer so many festivals all the year round. Whatever the time of year, someone somewhere in Singapore is sure to be celebrating. Here is a selection of the main events:

The **Chinese New Year** (Lunar New Year, January/February) is an occasion for merry-making that lasts for two weeks. The lion and dragon dances and the Chingay Parade of musicians, acrobats and dancers are the highlights. The first two days are official holidays and many of the streets and squares are decorated with coloured lights, oil lamps and *papier-mâché* figures.

By New Year's Day, houses and flats must be cleaned and all debts paid and, from then on, a new creature from the Chinese astrological year influences fortunes. Envelopes with money *(hong bao)* – or at least symbolic money – are distributed and guests present their hosts with mandarin oranges as presents.

Thaipusam (January/February) is a day of repentance for Hindus. A highlight of the festival occurs in the afternoon when the devotees express their faith to Lord Subramaniam by sticking hooks and metal spikes into their skin and then walking the 3km (2 miles) route from Sri Srinivasa Perumal Temple in Serangoon Road to the Sri Thandayuthapani Temple (also known as Chettiar Temple) in Tank Road.

Birthday of the Monkey God (February/March and September/October) is celebrated by the Chinese twice a year. During the celebrations, the spirit of the Monkey God enters into mediums, who skewer their cheeks and tongues with spikes and write charms in their own blood.

Monkey God birthday celebration

Ramadan (date varies annually), the month when Moslems fast, is the best time of year to sample Malay delicacies. Around the Sultan Mosque *(see page 43)* area and Geylang Serai *(see page 50)*, numerous stalls are set up to sell tasty offerings when Moslems break their fast after sunset. Ramadan ends with a grand festival, the **Hari Raya Puasa**, when friends and family meet for a lavish meal.

The **Qing Ming Festival** (April) is the Chinese equivalent of All Souls' Day. The Chinese clean ancestral graves and take food and other offerings to the cemeteries.

Hari Raya Haji (May) is a day which Moslems spend in prayer, remembering those who are making a pilgrim-

Buddha and a follower

age to Mecca. Animals are slaughtered in the late afternoon near the Sultan Mosque and the meat is then distributed to the needy.

Vesak Day (May) is a sacred day for Buddhists. It is the day when devout Buddhists celebrate the birth, enlightenment and death of Buddha with fervent prayer and by making offerings in the temples (e.g. Temple of the Thousand Lights, *see page 41*). The festival begins with traditional chants and then birds are released from their cages, a gesture that Buddhists hope will bring salvation. A candle light procession concludes the day.

The **Dragon Boat Festival** (June) consists mainly of a boat race in which participants from all over the world take part. The event is dedicated to the Chinese poet and statesman Qu Yuan. Over 2,500 years ago, he drowned himself in protest against corruption and injustice. According to legend, fishermen rushed into the water to save him and by beating drums and thrashing the water they stopped the fish from devouring him. In today's races, the sound of wild drumbeats precedes the racing boats.

The **Singapore Food Festival** (1–31 July) allows food lovers to indulge themselves in a way unimaginable at other times of the year. Gourmets are invited to sample new dishes that restaurant chefs have devised.

At the **Festival of the Hungry Ghost** (July/August) a feast is provided for the hungry spirits of dead Chinese. Throughout the city, food is left in bowls for the dead. The financial needs of the dead are also met by providing imitation bank notes and credit cards. The living enjoy themselves by watching one of the Chinese operas that are performed in Chinatown and on many of the estates, sometimes twice a day.

National Day (9 August), celebrating independence, appeals to the patriotism of Singaporeans. Folk groups, schools, music groups, social clubs and the military all take part in parades in the Padang (*see page 23*) or National Stadium. You need tickets, which are always in short supply. A laser and firework display ends the day.

The **Mooncake Festival** (September/October at the time of the full moon) recalls the victory of the Chinese over the Mongols courtesy of Zhu Yuan Zhang, who outwitted the hated occupying forces with messages hidden in little cakes. Children parade with lanterns and everyone eats pastries filled with lotus seeds, red bean paste and salted egg yolk.

Navarathiri (September/October) is Tamil for *nine nights*. This festival honours supreme goddess Devi with three nights devoted to each incarnation: Durga, Lakshmi and Saraswathi. You can hear classical Indian music and watch traditional dancing. The Chettiar Temple in Tank Road is a good place to see the performances (*see page 55*).

Thimithi (September/October) is a Hindu festival in honour of the goddess Draupadai. At the Sri Mariamman Temple (*see page 32*) men run barefoot across glowing embers. For a good view, it is best to arrive early.

Pilgrimage to Kusu Island (September/October/November). Chinese Taoists pay their respects at the Tua Pekong Temple on the island of Kusu where legend says a giant turtle saved a shipwrecked Malay and Chinese from drowning by turning itself into the island.

Deepavali (October/November), or the Festival of Lights, celebrates the victory of light over darkness. Serangoon Road is the focal point for the festivities. Garlands brighten Little India by day and illuminations by night. Restaurants and food stalls serve special delicacies.

Deepavali illuminations

The **Festival of the Nine Emperor Gods** (October/November) lasts nine days. Colourful processions and Chinese opera honour the gods so they will heal the sick and grant long life. The Kiu Ong Yiah Temple in Upper Serangoon Road is at the centre of the festivities.

Christmas lights (November to January) brighten Orchard Road for weeks, and hotels and shopping centres compete for the best decorated building. Although only 14 percent of Singaporean are Christian, many are crazy about Christmas and giving presents is an accepted custom.

Mooncake Festival magic

Food and Drink

A fact always well understood by lovers of fine food, has now been recognised by tourists: Singapore has many culinary attractions. In the multi-racial melting pot, all the various Asian cuisines compete in the battle of the taste buds: Chinese, Indonesian, Malaysian, Indian, Thai, Japanese, Korean, Arab. The choice is further complicated because Hokkien Chinese cooking is quite different from Cantonese and southern Indians like their food hotter than their countrymen further north.

The choice of restaurants is vast, and even dyed-in-the-wool consumers of European food will not be disappointed. Pasta and pizza parlours abound, alongside French *haute cuisine* restaurants and burger bars. It is easy to eat well and cheaply in Singapore. In every shopping centre stalls serve quick food at a reasonable price.

Dining options

The prices of meals in the restaurants of luxury hotels are on a par with international levels, but alcohol, particularly wine, will push the price up quite dramatically. Even a bottle of the local beer (Anchor, Tiger) – certainly as good as an imported beer – will add about six dollars to the bill. To save money, do what the Singaporeans do and drink water or tea. Both are usually provided free of charge with the meal.

71

Three important tips: 'hot' means really hot, 'spicy' is milder, but still hot; smoking is forbidden in air-conditioned restaurants (and pubs that serve food); 14 percent is added for service and tax; waiters do not expect a tip.

The descriptions of the various cuisines that follow include recommendations for relevant speciality restaurants, listed according to three categories: $$$ = expensive; $$ = moderate; $ = inexpensive.

Nonya cooking

Nonya cooking grew out of the first Chinese-Malay marriages. The menfolk did not wish to give up their favourite dishes and certainly not pork, which is excluded from all Malay recipes because of strict Moslem rules. Nonya food usually consists of Chinese ingredients, such as certain vegetables, and meats like pork and duck, which are then prepared in the Malay style, often with chilli and coconut milk. *Otak-otak* for instance, a dish in which fish is wrapped in a banana leaf, is prepared in the typical Malay fashion. Generally, the food is hot and spicy with a high calorie count. Velvety coconut milk and sugar are certainly not spared in the preparation of sweet desserts. Unfortunately, only a few restaurants serve Nonya food.

$$**Nonya and Baba**, 262 River Valley Road, tel: 734 1382.
$$**Peranakan Inn**, 210 East Coast Road, tel: 440 6195.

Chinese cooking

Don't be surprised if a Chinese greets you with 'Have you eaten?' and not 'How are you?'. To say that you have a full stomach is like saying 'I'm fine'. For the Chinese, eating is probably the most important thing in the world. In the words of an old Chinese proverb: 'Everything that moves with its back to the sun is edible'.

Most people will recognize the items on Chinese menus: spring rolls or prawn noodle soup for starters, followed perhaps by Peking duck, served with bean sprouts and fried rice. The dessert menu will almost certainly include almond-scented longan jelly and mango pudding. To be a little more adventurous try shark's fin soup, chilli crab or bird's nest. Eating bird's nest may seem unattractive, but what is eaten is the hardened, glue-like slime that binds the nest. Before eating, all leaves and grasses are removed. The rather bland taste in no way justifies the huge price (up to S\$150 per portion).

Hawker-stall dining

On two matters all Chinese agree. It is improper to gesticulate with chopsticks or point them at anyone, and rice or noodles form an essential part of any meal. After that, the tastes of the various Chinese regions drift apart. Almost all the regions are represented in Singapore, but most of the Chinese originate from the southern provinces.

Hokkien cooking

The largest dialect group has very little to boast about in gastronomic terms, and few restaurants serve Hokkien cuisine. Pork is popular – with plenty of fat. Hokkien Chinese like rich, satisfying food. Soups are served with vegetables and meatballs. Fried *hokkien mee*, is popular – a wholesome noodle dish with vegetables, meat, fish and garlic in a creamy sauce. It is the unofficial national dish of Singapore and can be enjoyed at many food stalls.
\$\$–\$\$\$Beng Thin Hoon Kee, OCBC Centre (5th floor), 65 Chulia Street, tel: 533 2818. **\$\$Beng Hiang**, 112 Amoy Street, tel: 221 6684.

Cantonese cooking

Cantonese is many people's favourite – perhaps because it is always elegantly presented, as, for example, in Hong Kong, where the exquisite 'little hearts' *(dim sum)*, are served for lunch. Shark's fin soup is another famous Cantonese dish. Wealthier inhabitants of the old province of Canton did not eat to build up their strength for work in the fields, they ate for enjoyment. So the food is often light with delicate and imaginative seasonings, which bring out the full natural aroma and taste of the ingredients, meat and seafood in particular.
\$\$\$Hung Kang Restaurant, 38 North Canal Road, tel: 533 5300. The best place for shark's fin soup. **\$\$–\$\$\$Mitzi**

Cantonese Restaurant, 24/26 Murray Street, tel: 222
8281. **$$–$$$Wang Jiang Lou**, Clarke Quay (Merchants
Court, #01-09), tel: 433 0166. **$$Lee Tong Kee**, 278 South
Bridge Road (near Sago Street). Well-known for its *dim
sum* and noodle soups.

Teochew cooking

The recipes of the second-largest dialect group concen-
trate on lighter, easily digestible foods. Many Teochew
Chinese earned their living from fishing, so the dishes tend
to be mainly seafood. Particularly popular are the fishballs
made from finely chopped fish, salt and water that are
added to soups and noodles. Another Teochew special-
ity which all Singaporeans enjoy for breakfast is a kind
of porridge made from fish, meat or vegetables.
$$Teochew Garden, 68 Orchard Road (Plaza Singapura,
#03-13), tel: 338 3661. **$–$$Ban Seng**, 79 New Bridge
Road, tel: 533 1471.

Hakka cooking

Hakka food can be described as simple and undemanding,
just like the lives of the old Hakka nomads in China. Soya
bean curd often replaces meat and, instead of fresh vegetables, ingredients preserved in salt are added to many
dishes. Nevertheless, the rather basic food is still very tasty.
Try *yong tau foo*, a soya bean curd with chopped meat.
$–$$Moi Kong, 22 Murray Street, tel: 221 7758.

73

Hawker food can be very tasty

Sichuan cooking

For centuries, strong spices have been used in the western
province of China. Chilli, the stronger the better, has always been a favourite, but take care with the dried, red
chillies that are served in restaurants. These can burn the
tongue and cause considerable discomfort. Try one of
the typical fried dishes with chicken or prawns served with
whole, dried chilli pods.
$$–$$$Golden Phoenix (in the Hotel Equatorial), Bukit
Timah Road, tel: 732 0431. **$$–$$$Dragon City**, 214
Dunearn Road (Novotel Orchid), tel: 254 7070.

Beijing cooking

The delicious crispy skin of the Peking Duck, rolled in thin
pancakes with a sauce and spring onions, is a famous Beijing speciality, usually served as an appetiser. The duck
meat and vegetables follow as the second course. Only
then is the duck soup served. But duck is not the only meat
on offer. Excellent lamb and mutton dishes are also very
popular. These were brought to Beijing many years ago
by Moslems from neighbouring Mongolia and Manchuria.
$$–$$$Pine Court, Orchard Road (Mandarin Hotel, 36th
floor), tel: 737 4411.

Hainan cooking

It is said that Hainan has borrowed heavily from western cooking. Chicken rice, for example, involves cooking the fowl slowly and then adding rice to the stock. A chilli-garlic sauce gives extra flavour. The Hainan invented the steamboat, a type of fondue where everyone cooks their food in a communal pot filled with stock. When ready, the morsels are dipped in various sauces.

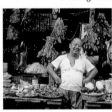
Fresh greens

$$–$$$Charming Garden (in the Novotel Orchid), 214 Dunearn Road, tel: 251 8149. **$$Swee Kee Restaurant**, 51 Middle Road, tel: 338 6986.

Herbal cooking

The Chinese live to eat, so they take their food very seriously. The effect of certain food and food combinations have been studied in China for centuries. The concern of many cooks is to create a balanced diet, so that the *yin* (cooling) and *yang* (warming) balance the body. Such a diet will also taste good, but that is a pleasant side effect. It is not easy for the layman to tell *yin* from *yang* foods and know which herbs have healing powers.

$$$Imperial Herbal Restaurant (Metropole Hotel), 41 Sea Street, tel: 337 0491.

Vegetarian cooking

A diet without meat might seem to suit the Chinese preoccupation with food and health but, apart from strict Buddhists, few Chinese are vegetarians. One reason may be that Chinese shun raw food, although soya-bean curd and other vegetarians' favourites form part of the Chinese diet. Nevertheless, there are many restaurants (some Indian) that prepare imaginative vegetarian dishes.

$$–$$$Bombay Woodlands, Tanglin Road (Tanglin Shopping Centre), tel: 235 2712. **$$Kamats**, 147 Serangoon Road, tel: 291 7930 (Indian/vegetarian). **$$Fut Sai Kai**, 147 Kitchener Road, tel: 298 0336. **$$Loke Woh Yuen Vegetarian Restaurant**, 20 Tanjong Pagar Road, tel: 221 2912.

Seafood

Singapore is an island, so fresh fish and seafood have always played an important part in the native diet. Nowadays, what is not available close at hand, is imported, e.g. large crabs from Sri Lanka and giant lobsters from Thailand. Most of the seafood restaurants are concentrated around the East Coast Parkway.

Seafood is everywhere

Fish and crustaceans are usually boiled or grilled. Drunken prawns is an unusual dish where the prawns are brought to the table in a bowl of alcohol. When the little creatures are 'drunk', the spirit is lit. Far more appetising is chilli crab – the large crabs are coated in a creamy, fiery-hot sauce. Crispy, fried baby squid served with a dark soya sauce is another delicious speciality.

East Coast Recreation Centre (by the Big Splash swimming pool), East Coast Parkway (*see Route 8, page 52*): **$$$Seafood Palace**, tel: 442 0988; **$$$Seafood International**, tel: 345 1211. UDMC **Seafood Centre**, East Coast Parkway: $$–$$$**Long Beach Seafood**, tel: 445 8833; $$**New Kheng Luck**, tel: 442 2690.

UDMC Seafood centre

Malay and Indonesian cooking

Malays have skilfully combined the cooking methods of their northern and southern neighbours, the Thais and the Indonesians. Many dishes are enriched with thick coconut milk sauces or hot chillies. Lemon grass and curry also play a part in Malay cuisine as do coriander and meat. Fish is as popular as meat and chicken, but Moslems will not eat pork. *Satay*, small kebabs of marinated meat, are very popular, especially when grilled over charcoal and served with a spicy peanut sauce. Malays and Indonesians do not use chopsticks.

Geylang Serai Market

Malay
$$$Aziza's, 180 Albert Street, #02-15 Albert Court, tel: 235 1130. $$–$$$**House of Sundanese Food**, 55 Boat Quay, tel: 535 3775 (closed Sunday) and 218 East Coast Road, tel: 345 5020 (closed Monday). $$**Bintang Timur Restaurant**, 14 Scotts Road (Far East Plaza), #03–08, tel: 235 4539.

Indonesian
$$**Seri Restu**, 23A Lorong Mambong (Holland Village), tel: 466 4311. $–$$**Sanur Indonesian**, Orchard Road (Centrepoint Shopping Centre, #04–17), tel: 734 2192. $–$$**Tambuah Mas**, Tanglin Road (Tanglin Shopping Centre, #04–10), tel: 733 3333.

Indian cooking

South Indian food, the sort more likely to be encountered in Singapore, is much hotter than North Indian food. Some dishes may be too hot for western palates, in which case ask for a mild main course. Yoghurt accompanies most meals and can help tone down spiciness.

Southern Indian dishes usually come with rice; in the north, more bread is eaten. The *roti prata* or soft pancakes from the south are quite delicious for breakfast, but *chapatis* and *naans* from the north accompany all meals. *Dosai* are south Indian specialities, shaped from rice dough and served with curries.

Southern Indian curries are enriched with coconut milk and are consequently thicker than northern curries. Fish head curry is a Singaporean creation and should not be missed. North Indians often use the clay *tandoor* oven for cooking meat, chicken and fish and tandoori chicken has become very popular in recent years. Also worth a try is *jeenga tandoori dilbahar*, marinated prawns baked in the *tandoor*.

South Indian
$$–$$$Banana Leaf Apollo, 56 Race Course Road, tel: 293 8682. **$$–$$$Muthu's Curry Restaurant**, 78 Race Course Road, tel: 293 7029. **$$Komala Vilas**, 76 Serangoon Road, tel: 293 6980. **$$–$$$Madras New Woodlands**, 12-14 Upper Dickson Road, tel: 297 1594. **$$ $$$Nagoraar Restaurant**, 147 Telok Ayer Street *(see Route 3, page 34)*, tel: 226 3614. Large selection of *roti*

Shopping for fresh ingredients

prata dishes. **$–$$Zam Zam**, 699 North Bridge Road (corner of Arab Street), tel: 298 7011.

North Indian
$$The Tandoor, 11 Cavenagh Road (Holiday Inn Park View basement), tel: 733 8333. **$$Delhi Restaurant**, 60 Race Course Road, tel: 296 4585. **$$Moti Mahal**, 18 Murray Street (Food Alley), tel: 221 4338. **$$–$$$Orchard Maharajah**, 25 Cuppage Terrace, tel: 732 6331 (also al fresco). **$$Kinara**, 61 Boat Quay, tel: 533 0412.

Other Asian cuisines
Almost every nation on the Asian continent is represented in Singapore. Many wealthy Japanese visit the island, so there is now an abundance of *sushi* bars and *teppanyaki* restaurants. These traditional Japanese foods will cost much less than in Tokyo or Osaka and the raw fish that is used in Singapore will also be much fresher. *Sushi* has recently caught on in Singapore and now lots of fast food stalls specialise in these dainty little rolls as well as more traditional Japanese fare such as noodle soup.

Japanese
$$$Unkai, ANA Hotel, 16 Nassim Hill, tel: 732 1222. **$$Hoshigaoka**, 435 Orchard Road (Wisma Atria Shopping Centre, #01-18), tel: 734 2546. Economical family restaurant with accessible menu and interesting displays.

Thai
$$–$$$Chao Phaya, Thai Seafood Market & Restaurant, Ang Mo Kio Avenue 6 (Ang Mo Kio Shopping Centre, Block 730, #02-4272), tel: 453 7271. **$$Bann Thai Restaurant**, Ngee Ann City, Tower A, #04–23, tel: 735 5563.

International cooking
Almost all large hotels have restaurants serving western fare. These establishments are not just where homesick expatriates congregate; they also attract tourists bemused by the wealth of foods on offer. Given the wide choice

of good quality ingredients available in Singapore, it is easy for western chefs to serve up the juicy steaks, fresh vegetables and delicate fish dishes, much loved by Europeans and Americans.

The **Duxton** and the **Regent** (*see Accommodation*) have very popular international restaurants as does the **Alkaff Mansion** which is well-known for its *rijstaffel* (*see Further Sights, page 55*). **Pasta Fresca** has a branch by the Boat Quay and **Delifrance**, ideal for breakfast or a snack during the day, has outlets in the city centre. Many global fast-food chains have opened branches in Singapore.

Alkaff Mansion restaurant

Raffles

Staying in the Raffles Hotel may be out of reach for many tourists, but eating there is a different matter. Two restaurants, the French-style **Raffles Grill** and the Asian **Tiffin Room**, are in the main hotel wing, but four other restaurants are located in the white-painted, two-storey arcade of the exclusive shopping centre: the elegant **Empress Room** serving Cantonese food, **Ah Teng's Bakery** for baguettes, croissants and banana cakes served with cappuccino or jasmin tea, the **Seah Street Deli**, an American-inspired meeting place serving ready-to-eat snacks and meals and finally the **Empire Café** where Singaporean dishes are available. **Raffles Courtyard** is a great place for a late-afternoon drink, while lunch in the **Bar and Billiard Room** can be a lavish affair. In the evening, try a Singapore Sling in the **Long Bar**.

77

Singapore Sling

This now famous drink was first prepared in 1915 by Ngiam Tong Boon, a barman in the original Raffles Hotel. It tastes dangerously fruity and first timers may be lulled into thinking that it contains no alcohol. But that is certainly not the case. The recipe is no longer a secret: 5cl gin, 3cl pineapple juice, 1cl fresh lemon juice, a shot of Benedictine, a shot of Cointreau, a little cherry brandy. Shake well with ice and then pour into a long glass half-full of ice. Top up with soda water and decorate with fruit. Cheers!

The durian fruit

Many of the tropical fruit available in Singapore give off a pleasant aroma, but the durian fruit stinks to high heaven. For the locals though, it is the 'king of fruits'. Beneath the spiny, browny-green skin, this tree fruit, which is as big as a rugby ball, actually contains some delicious, soft, white flesh. Many tourists hold their noses when they pass the market stalls selling durian, but the Singaporeans will give them a good sniff. It is important to check that the fruit is fully ripe. Good durian fruit are really filling, but

The 'king of fruits'

their taste is difficult to describe. It is perhaps the creamy texture that is so appealing. Anyone wishing to sample without buying can do so at the Four Seasons by Clarke Quay. Taking durians home as a souvenir is definitely not recommended as they are banned by all hotels, all airlines and by the public transport authorities.

Hawker centres

Hawker centres, a cheap option

Sometimes called hawkers, these mobile food stands started out selling snacks from the roadside. Over the years, and with a little encouragement from the government, they formed into hawker centres and they have since become Singapore's favourite (and cheapest) source of fast food. It is hard to imagine how Singaporeans could survive without the hawker centres. Children eat there at the end of school, and their parents come when they have finished work. Every type of Asian food is available, and that means practically anything that can be prepared quickly – all at incredibly low prices. Choices include char-grilled *satays*, Indian mutton soup from a large pot or wok-fried Hong Kong noodles.

78

Lau Pa Sat mural

Try **Lau Pa Sat Festival Market** in the heart of the business quarter (Shenton Way/Boon Tat Street), one of the shopping centres in Orchard Road or in Chinatown (e.g. opposite Murray Terrace on Maxwell Road). There is a highly recommended hawker centre on Sentosa Island too.

Popular restaurant quarters

Food Alley (Murray Terrace) in Chinatown is a safer bet than the **Bugis quarter**, where the restaurants and small hawker stalls are rather mediocre in quality. By far the best choice of Asian and European restaurants is by the **Boat Quay** (between Cavanagh Bridge and South Bridge Road). Beware of the 'Wine and Dine Passport' – it bestows no price reductions on the user and only narrows the choice.

Clarke Quay: **$$$J.P. Bastiani Mediterranean Bar & Restaurant** (Merchant's Court, tel: 433 0156) has a good Italian menu and a pleasant atmosphere. Try also **$$$Key Largo Oyster Bar and Seafood Restaurant** (Trader's Market, tel: 334 40 55). In the **$$Steam Boat Restaurant** (Merchant's Court, no reservations) you prepare your own meal al fresco. The **Four Seasons** (Trader's Market) is a good place to try durians. Try hot stone meals, e.g. steaks served on hot stone, on the **Tongkangs** (old cargo boats).

For those who prefer not to stray too far from Orchard Road, **Cuppage Terrace** offers the best in outdoor dining. There is also a good selection of restaurants in the **Ngee Ann City Shopping Centre** (Orchard Road).

Shopping

Orchard Road is still Singapore's main shopping street, but it is worth making a detour into Scotts Road and Tanglin Road (*see Route 2*). Prices drop a little after Chinese New Year in February, and all shops take part in the Great Singapore Sale in July and August. Most shops are open Monday to Saturday 9.30am–9pm. Shops open on Sunday on Orchard Road.

Tanglin Mall

Shopping tips

In the markets and some shopping centres (e.g. Lucky Plaza on Orchard Road and in Chinatown) haggling is accepted. In the boutiques and department stores along Orchard Road, however, you pay the fixed price. Shops with merlion stickers are members of the city-run Good Retailer Scheme (GRS). GST (goods and service tax) at 3 percent is added, but if more than S$500 is spent in one shop displaying the tax refund logo, ask for a refund form. Show the goods at a counter in the airport and the GST will be refunded within 12 weeks.

Check that electrical goods will run on your home electricity, and for all electrical goods and cameras make sure the manufacturer's international guarantee card is enclosed (it tends to raise the price a little). If a shop agrees to send an item to your home, obtain written confirmation.

Visitors can take complaints either to the Singapore Tourist Board (*see page 90*) or the Consumers' Association of Singapore, Bukit Merah Central, Block 164 (#04-3625), tel: 270 5433, fax: 270 6786). If the disputed sum is less than S$2,000, the Small Claims Court (The Registrar, Old Ministry of Labour Building, Havelock Road, tel: 535 2692, 435 5937; S$10 fee) will resolve the issue within 48 hours.

Some trinkets to take home

Antiques

Katong Antique House, Peter Wee, 208 East Coast Road (tel: 345 8544 for an appointment).

Books

MPH **Stamford/Armenian Street**. Three storeys full of books, plus a café. Daily, 10am–9.30pm.
Select Books, 19 Tanglin Road, Tanglin Shopping Centre, #03-15. Monday to Saturday, 10am–9.30pm. Comprehensive selection of southeast Asian literature.

Computers

Funan Centre, North Bridge Road, by the Singapore River. All PCs have American keyboards and the software is usually written in English. The four upper storeys are large, electronic games rooms.

Fashions and accessories

Look along **Orchard Road** and **Tanglin Road** (*see Route 2*), in the **Raffles Hotel Arcades** and in the **Capitol Building** on Stamford Road.

Hi-fi/audio

Sim Lim Square (corner of Rochor Canal and Bencoolen Street), **Adelphi** (corner of Coleman Road and North Bridge Road) and **Plaza Singapura** (Orchard Road).

Jewellery

The determined haggler may get about S$800 knocked off the price of a S$4,500 Rolex watch at the well-stocked clock and watch shop **Thong Hiap** (51 Bras Basah Road). Fake watches are illegal. For unusual jewellery, try the **Tanglin Shopping Centre** and the **Raffles Hotel Arcade** (very expensive). The **Zhujiao Centre** in Little India (Serangoon Road) has a big selection of gold jewellery. To get gold and other jewellery checked, use the **Singapore Assay Office** (tel: 660 7330, fax: 261 2617).

The Raffles Arcade

80

Made-to-measure tailoring

A tailor given 48 hours can produce a wearer-designed suit. A silk suit will cost US$300–1,000.
Men: **Coloc Creation**, 218 Orchard Road (Orchard Emerald, #03-05), tel: 732 8968. **Justmen's Shop** (Tanglin Shopping Centre, #01-36), tel: 737 4800.
Women: **Peggy's Silk House**, Forum Galleria (basement), tel: 734 2725. **Miss Ming**, 333 Orchard Road, Mandarin Hotel Shopping Centre, #02–06 and 400 Orchard Road, Orchard Towers (opposite the Hilton), #01–26. Daily, 10am–7pm, one of the best places for Thai silk. **China Silk House**, Tanglin Shopping Centre, #02–11.

Photographic equipment

The **People's Park Complex** and **Chinatown Point** offer the cheapest prices. Try also **Lucky Plaza** in Orchard Road, the **Far East Shopping Centre** in Scotts Road and the **Far East Plaza** in Orchard Road. Haggling is acceptable in these shops. **Centrepoint** in Orchard Road also has a good selection of shops. **Goh Kin Camera Service** (Orchard Plaza, #02–37, tel: 732 6155. Monday to Saturday, 11am– 6.30pm) offers a quick camera repair service.

Decorative art at Ming Village

Porcelain

Ming Village, 32 Pandan Road, tel: 265 7711. 9am– 5.30pm. Take the 78 bus from Clementi MRT station and then it is a further 10-minute walk (*see Jurong, page 49*). **The Cannery** (#01–36) by Clarke Quay is a small shop selling Ming porcelain.

Souvenirs

The ground floor of the **Raffles Hotel Arcade** can supply something out of the ordinary – perhaps a cookery book containing the best recipes of top Asian restaurants.

Design Centre, 141 North Bridge Road (2nd floor), tel: 336 2766. 10am–7pm. Ideas from all over the world.

Say Tian Hng Buddha Shop, 35 Neil Road, tel: 221 1042. 10am–6pm. Deities and religious artefacts.

The Old Thong Chai Building (Seiwaen Arts Centre), 50 Eu Tong Seng Street, tel: 532 6311. *Objets d'art* in an old hospital.

National Museum Shop, 53 Armenian Street. Tasteful souvenirs, jewellery and books.

Hats and things

Fong Moon Kee, 16 Sago Street, tel: 223 0940. Monday to Saturday, 9am–6pm. Huge selection of body oils.

Art House, 198A Telok Ayer Street *(see Route 3, page 34)*, tel: 323 5572. Chinese opera costume hire. You can be dressed, made up and photographed (from S$35).

Lim's Arts & Crafts, 211 Holland Avenue (Holland Shopping Centre).

Singapore Philatelic Bureau, 1 Killiney Street (opposite the Orchard Plaza on Orchard Road). An eldorado for stamp collectors.

Tea

Tea Chapter, 9A Neil Road, tel: 226 1175. 11am–11pm. *(see page 36)*. An entrance fee of S$4.50 per person is charged but this is subtracted from the price of a drink. The Tea Chapter, where the Queen was once a visitor, can only be visited barefoot. **Yixing Xuan Tea House** (23 Neil Road, 11am–11pm) has a large selection of teas and tea sets.

Shopping centres away from Orchard Road

Chinatown *(see Route 3, page 32–37)*, **Little India** *(see Route 4, pages 38–41)* and **Arab Street** *(see Route 5, pages 42–43)* are popular shopping areas, together with **Marina Square** by the Marina Mandarin, Pan Pacific, Oriental and Ritz Carlton hotels and **Clarke Quay**.

Arab Street baskets

The best time to explore shophouses by the Singapore River is afternoon or early evening when the 100 or so shops are all open. The **Fu Lou Shou Centre** by Rochor Road (MRT station: Bugis Street) is very popular with the locals. A few traders, such as Master Tan the Feng Shui consultant, have moved here from nearby Bugis Street.

Markets

The oldest Singapore markets are found in **Geylang Serai** *(see Route 8, pages 50–52)*, **Chinatown** (Chinatown Complex, *see Route 3, pages 32–37*) and **Little India** *(see Route 4, pages 38–41)*.

Nightlife

Singapore's nightlife hit its stride at the beginning of the '90s. Boat Quay and Clarke Quay were restored and several large discos opened up beside the Singapore River. Now the city pulsates well into the early hours.

Eating out and going to discos is not cheap in Singapore. A glass of wine will cost S$7–10 and at weekends a cover charge is often levied in discos. Entrance charges, including a drink, vary around S$10–25. Many pubs have a happy hour around 5–8pm.

Most Singaporeans go out only at weekends, so that is when the bars and discos are full and the karaoke bars around Tanjong Pagar come alive. For a quieter, romantic evening, try the interesting Musical Fountain on Sentosa Island (from 7.30pm) or a cruise on a junk around the illuminated harbour with the glittering backdrop of the Singapore skyline (Watertours, tel: 533 9811, daily from 6.30pm, about 2½ hours, dinner included). For the best view of the city at night, visit the **Compass Rose Bar** in the Westin Stamford Hotel (*see page 26*).

Night lights on Bugis Street

There is always a lot happening in **Chinatown** (around Duxton Road/Tanjong Pagar), on **Bugis Street** (night market/restaurants), **Cuppage Terrace** (restaurants and pubs near Orchard Road) or at the **Lau Pa Sat Festival Market**. The **Adventure Ride** on Clarke Quay is a fantastic, ten-minute boat trip Disney-style along an 'artificial' Singapore River (open daily 10am–10pm, 3E River Valley Road, #01–13, tel: 337 1680). An evening stroll along the **Boat Quay** by Singapore River can be a relaxing way to end a day's sightseeing.

Ask the hotel reception for the current *Singapore Visitor* or look in the *Straits Times*, Singapore's daily newspaper. The tourist office will provide information on evening performances of Chinese opera (*wayang*).

Dinner shows

Singa Inn Seafood Restaurant, 920 East Coast Parkway (by the Big Splash leisure pool), tel: 345 1111. The 40-minute Asian Cultural Show (Monday to Friday, 8pm) is free, but guests must order an à la carte meal.

The best bars

Brannigan's, Hyatt Regency Singapore, 10–12 Scotts Road, tel: 733 1188. A 'yuppie' hang-out.

Harry's Quayside Café, 28 Boat Quay, tel: 538 3029. A favourite Caucasian hangout.

Hard Rock Café, 50 Cuscaden Road, tel: 235 5232. As popular as anywhere else in the world.

Flag & Whistle, 10 Duxton Hill, tel: 223 1126. For karaoke fans (closed Monday).

Saxaphone Bar & Restaurant, 23 Cuppage Road (Cuppage Terrace), tel: 235 8385. For European jazz fans.

Bar & Billiard Room, Raffles Hotel Arcade, 1 Beach Road, tel: 337 1886. Stylish restaurant that has become a refined 'après dinner' meeting-place – with billiard table.

The Long Bar (Raffles Hotel Arcade). Home of the Singapore sling and the only place in Singapore where there is no fine for throwing litter on the floor. Peanuts in shells are provided for those in need of catharsis.

Elvis Place, 298 Beach Road, The Concourse, Basement 1, #01-13, tel: 299 8403. Elvis souvenirs and plenty of 1950s music.

Party Doll, Shophouse Row, 3D River Valley Road, #03–01/02, Clarke Quay, tel: 339 3139. Live bands and music from the 1950s and '60s.

Anywhere, 19 Tanglin Road, #04–08/09, Tanglin Shopping Centre, tel: 734 8233. Reputation for good live music (closed Sunday).

The best discos

The Warehouse, River View Hotel, 382 Havelock Road, tel: 732 9922. Discotheque in an old warehouse by the Singapore River.

Fire Discotheque, 150 Orchard Road, #04–19 Orchard Plaza, tel: 235 0155. Dance floors on two storeys.

Sparks, Level 8, Ngee Ann City, 391 Orchard Road, tel: 732 6133. Another popular dance hall.

Top Ten, 400 Orchard Road, #04–35 Orchard Towers, tel: 732 3077. Used to be a cinema. Now Singapore's most successful disco.

Zouk/Velvet Underground, 17, 19 & 21 Jiak Kim Street (corner of Kim Seng Road), tel: 738 2988. Not just a disco, but also a wine bar. In an old warehouse. Closed Monday.

Tanjong Pagar and Boat Quay

Getting There

Opinion polls have consistently shown that air travellers rate Changi Airport very highly and with justification. Sometimes referred to as an 'Airtropolis', the terminals here have seen annual passenger numbers rise to 24 million. The signposting is excellent and it is stated in the regulations that the first piece of luggage must be on the carousel within 12 minutes of a plane's arrival. With the comfortable cafés, pianists, waterfalls, video walls, cinema, electronic games hall and very good selection of shops, waiting time passes quickly. The airport is equipped with a professional Business Centre (3rd floor, 8.30am–10pm), three post and telephone counters and several banks. Money changing facilities are available immediately on arrival.

At the moment, there are two terminals, linked by a free 'skytrain'. Singapore Airlines, one of the most profitable airlines in the world, is based in Terminal 2, together with Swissair, Philippine Airlines, Air France, Silkair and Malaysia Airlines. All other airlines use Terminal 1.

Two hotels in the airport offer day rooms (about S\$55 for six hours, tel: 0065/545 8365, fax: 0065/542 3828, Terminal 1, or tel: 0065/543 0911, Terminal 2). Air passengers should remember to put a swimming costume in their in-flight luggage, as they are allowed to use the swimming pool, situated by Terminal 1's Sky Train station. Open: 7am–8pm, free for hotel guests. Passengers with a stopover wait of more than four hours are entitled to a sightseeing tour of the city (daily, 10.30am, 2.30 and 4.30pm).

Transfer to the city centre by taxi is never a problem as sufficient taxis are always at hand. Fare: S\$20 including S\$3 airport supplement. Journey time: 30 minutes.

Singapore Airlines (SIA) connects Singapore with all the world's major cities.

An airport tax of S\$15 is due for return or onward flights and this can only be paid in the local currency. Some hotels sell the appropriate coupons at reception.

It is essential to confirm return flight times at least 72 hours before departure. This can be done at the appropriate airline office, either in person or by phone. Remember to have the reconfirmation code number to hand.

85

Changi Airtropolis

By sea

Arriving slowly by sea, as everyone was obliged to do in days gone by, is a pleasant experience. You sail in past 600 or so other vessels lying at anchor, watching the skyline clarify into looming skyscrapers. Most visitors arrive at one of the three terminals of the impressive Singapore Cruise Centre, which can accommodate up to 1,000 passengers at a time.

The MRT is spotless

Getting Around

Taxis and the superb public transport system are the best way of touring Singapore. The government uses a car entitlement system to keep private cars off the road.

MRT (Mass Rapid Transit) System

The air-conditioned underground stations are finished in marble, glass, chrome and stone. Their interiors are more reminiscent of large banks than stations on a busy public transport system, particularly as they are always clean and polished. The network extends for 83km (51 miles) and tickets cost between S$0.60 and 1.50. Keep the ticket, as it is needed to open and close the barrier at the station entrance and exit. A tourist ticket can be purchased for S$6. It may not reduce the cost of travelling but it does make a good souvenir. The Transit Link Ticket (S$12) is valid for the MRT and buses. Both this and the tourist ticket are available from all MRT stations. The cost of each journey is automatically deducted from the card. Singapore's underground network operates 6am–midnight and the ticket machines are easy to use. Smoking, eating and carrying durian fruit are forbidden.

Getting ahead

Buses

SBS and TIBS are the main bus companies. The bus route network is dense and services connect every corner of the island. More than half of the buses are air-conditioned. Fares range from S$ 0.50 to S$1.20. Always keep plenty of change handy or else buy a Singapore Explorer Ticket (available from hotels; S$5 for one day, S$12 for three days; city map showing all bus routes included). The **Singapore Trolley** also issues day passes (available from hotels; S$9). These old-fashioned trams run 9am–9pm at

30-minute intervals and cover all the main sights in the city centre. They also go to Sentosa island.

Taxis

More than 13,000 taxis use the streets of Singapore, but only on Friday and Saturday evening can it prove difficult to find one. The best advice on such occasions is to wait at a hotel entrance.

Most taxi-drivers are Chinese and they are not perhaps as cautious as their western passengers might like them to be, but fares are very reasonable. The basic charge is S$2.40 and this covers the first 1½ kilometres (1 mile); each additional 240m (260 yards) cost 10 cents. Fares rise by 50 percent in the period midnight–6am. Journeys that start inside the 'Restricted Zone' (Central Business District) cost an extra dollar. Daily area licences (S$3 per vehicle) are payable by the passenger, unless the taxi already displays a valid licence. Do not be alarmed if a bell rings inside the cab. It is a gentle reminder to the driver that he has exceeded the speed limit of 80 kmph (50 mph).

Trishaws are good for sightseeing

Trishaws

Trishaws are bicycles with sidecars. They are ideal for taking tourists on sightseeing trips, but are impractical as a means of transport. Fares must be paid in advance. Expect to pay S$20–30 per hour.

Boats

Wooden *bumboats* leave for boat trips on the Singapore River from the Raffles Landing Stage (*see Route 1, page 22*) and Chinese junks depart from Clifford Pier for day

Boats to Indonesia and the smaller islands off the main island leave from near the World Trade Centre (WTC). On the second floor of the WTC, a number of travel agents offer stand-by cruises or short trips (with accommodation) to Indonesia.

Sentosa

Entrance to Sentosa is S$5 per person (S$3 for children). There are additional charges for the various attractions. Access to hotels by taxi is free between 10pm and 7am, S$6 at other times. For information , tel: 743 8668.

Sentosa can be reached by ferry from the World Trade Centre (WTC), by cable car from the WTC or Mount Faber or across the causeway on foot or by bus or taxi.

The WTC is served by the Singapore Trolley (*see page 86*); bus Nos 97 or 167 from Shenton Way (Clifford Pier); and bus C from Tiong Bahru MRT station. Bus A goes from WTC as far as Underwater World. Ferries for the four-minute crossing to Sentosa depart every 20 minutes from the WTC's ground floor, daily 10am–9pm. Every 30 minutes a bus shuttle runs between Sentosa and the WTC.

From Tiong Bahru MRT station, bus B goes to Central Beach (every 10 minutes, Saturday and Sunday only, 8am–7pm). Bus E leaves from the Lucky Plaza shopping centre in Orchard Road.

The last bus leaves Sentosa at 11.30pm. If the taxi queue is too big, take the bus to Tiong Bahru MRT station then go by underground to the city centre and hail a taxi.

To Malaysia and Thailand

You can fly to Malaysia and Thailand from Changi. Anyone hiring a car to drive in Malaysia is advised to hire in Johor Bahru (*see Excursions, page 60*), rather than Singapore. To stop 'fuel tourism' the authorities insist tanks in hire cars leaving Singapore must be at least three-quarters full of the more expensive Singaporean fuel.

Several buses a day leave for Johor Bahru or Kuala Lumpur (Pan Malaysia Express Pte, on the corner of Kallang Bahru and Lavender Street, tel: 293 5915). Tickets must be purchased one day in advance.

Singapore does not have railway lines: the station in Keppel Road belongs to Malaysia. Six trains a day leave here for Kuala Lumpur (journey time: approx. 7 hours).

At the E&O

Twice a week, the ultra-expensive **Eastern & Oriental Express** journeys through jungle and plantations to Bangkok. The 1,943-km (1,204-mile) journey takes about 41 hours. Tel: 227 2068.

Every day at 7.50am a boat for Tioman in West Malaysia leaves from the World Trade Centre. Kelpin Tours, tel: 271 4866, fax: 273 3543.

Facts for the Visitor

Visas

Visitors do not need a visa prior to travel to Singapore, they will normally be given a two-week tourist visa on arrival. Those staying longer than 14 days in Singapore can extend their visa by applying to the Immigration Department by North Boat Quay, tel: 532 2877. Excursions to Indonesia and Malaysia do not require visas.

Customs

Duty-free goods (except cigarettes) can be bought on arrival in Singapore's Changi airport before passing through customs control. Cigarettes brought into Singapore attract a surcharge of S$17 per carton, regardless of where they were bought. It is possible to leave imported cigarettes with the Singaporean customs authorities and collect them when leaving the country.

Cigarettes may be bought in the airport duty-free shop before leaving. There are no export duties in Singapore and no limits for importing or exporting the Singapore dollar. Chewing gum may not be imported into Singapore, though small amounts for personal use are allowed.

Drug dealers and anyone caught in possession of drugs face the death penalty under Singapore law.

Travellers over the age of 18 may import 1 litre spirits and 1 litre wine duty-free. Pornographic magazines, videos and weapons (even blowpipes) may not be imported. For further information contact the Chief Customs Officer at Changi airport, tel: 541 2572.

Under the CITES agreement, the importation into Europe of animal skins, ivory, turtle shell, etc, is banned. If any of these items are found by customs officers, they will be confiscated and a heavy fine can be imposed.

Jungle rock

89

One for the album

Tourist information

The Singapore Tourist Promotion Board (STPB) keeps a large collection of brochures for potential visitors.

In the UK: 1st Floor, Carrington House, 126–130 Regent Street. London W1R 5FE, tel: 0171 437 0033, fax: 0171 734 2191.

In the US: 8484 Wilshire Boulevard, Suite 510, Beverly Hills, CA 90201, tel: 213 852 1901, fax: 213 852 0129; 590 Fifth Avenue, 12th Floor, New York, NY 10036, tel: 212 302 4861, fax: 212 302 4801; Two Prudential Plaza, 180 North Stetson Avenue, Suite 1450, Chicago, Illinois 60601, tel: 312 938 1883, fax: 312 938 0086.

In Hong Kong: Room 2003 Central Plaza, 18 Harbour Road, Wanchai, tel: 852 2598 9290, fax: 852 2598 1040.

In Singapore: 328 North Bridge Road, Raffles Hotel Arcade, #02-34, tel: 334 1335. Daily, 8.30am–8pm. A 24-hour free information service is available on 1 800 831 3311. STPB headquarters, Tourism Court, 1 Orchard Spring Lane, tel: 736 6622, fax: 736 9423. Daily, 8.30am–6pm.

Currency and exchange

Singapore's dollar (S$) consists of 100 cents. Money can be changed in banks, hotels and licensed *bureaux de change*. Credit cards are welcomed almost everywhere (Visa, Mastercard). It is also useful to take Travellers' Cheques. These can be changed at the Authorised Money Changers in the shopping centres – although a better rate is sometimes obtained at banks.

If problems arise with credit cards, ring 1 800 732 2244 (American Express), 1 800 225 5225 (Citibank/Visa), 1 800 292 7566 (Diners Card), 336 5277 (Hongkong Bank, Mastercard and Visa). Banks are open Monday to Friday, 10am–3pm and Saturday, 9.30–11am.

Public holidays

Details of the main festivals for the various ethnic groups are given in the section 'Festivals' (*see pages 67–9*). National holidays in Singapore are as follows: 1 January (New Year's Day), end of January/beginning of February (Chinese New Year), March/April (Good Friday), mid-March/beginning of April (Hari Raya Puasa, end of Ramadan), 1 May (Labour Day), 9 August (National Day), November (Deepavali, Hindu festival of light) and 25 December (Christmas).

Deepavali decoration

Telephone

Telephone calls are cheap. A three-minute local call from a public call box will cost about 10 cents.

To make an international call from a public telephone box, first get a phonecard from the post office or a telecom outlet. The cards come in S$ 2-, 10-, 20- or 50- denominations. Singapore's telecommunications network is of the highest standard. The Comcentre is open around the clock and you can hire a mobile phone for about S$20 per day. For further information, tel: 235 9595 or 543 0123.

For international calls from Singapore, dial 001, followed by 44 for the UK and 1 for the US or Canada. Remember to omit the 0 from the UK area code and then dial the required number. To call Singapore from overseas, dial for an international line followed by 65.

To seek assistance from the operator, tel: 104 or 161. For information, tel: 103.

Postal services

The General Post Office is situated in the Fullerton Building by Cavenagh Bridge. Open daily, 8am–8pm. Although situated on the 4th floor, the post office in the Ngee Ann City Shopping Centre by Orchard Road is in a convenient location. Monday to Saturday, 8am–8.30pm.

A postcard to Europe requires a 40 cent stamp. It will take a few days to arrive.

Time

Singapore is eight hours ahead of GMT.

Electricity

Electricity is at the UK standard 220V 50Hz.

Clothing

Pack light and loose-fitting clothes, preferably made of cotton, as the heat in Singapore can be oppressive. However, T-shirts and shorts are not really suitable for a walk in the city centre, as the air-conditioning units in shops and restaurants are often set to very cool temperatures and a thin jumper may be required.

Guaranteed delivery

91

Memories of Britain

Researching itineraries

Photography
Many shops offer a rapid film development service. Slide films (E6 process) can be developed at Standard Photo (565 MacPherson Road, tel: 282 22. Monday to Friday, 9am–6pm).

Language
English is understood practically everywhere. Malay, Mandarin and Tamil are the other official languages.

Tipping
Tipping in restaurants is not essential in Singapore, as a service charge, usually 10 percent, is included in the bill and shown as an extra. If it is not shown, then a tip of 10 percent will be acceptable.

Medical assistance
Medical provision in Singapore is excellent. The names of doctors are listed in the 'Yellow Pages' under 'Medical Practitioners'. Singapore General Hospital is in Outram Road, tel: 222 3322.

Good private insurance is advisable and should provide for every eventuality.

No inoculations are required for Singapore but, if a trip into Malaysia or Indonesia is planned, then anti-malaria tablets are recommended.

Water
Singapore's tap water is perfectly drinkable.

Disabled
It is generally quite easy for disabled people to get about in Singapore. The Singapore tourist office will supply a leaflet entitled 'The Physically Disabled Person's Guide to Accessible Places' and this provides information on disabled access to hotels and tourist sites.

Emergencies
Call 999 for police, 995 for ambulance and fire brigade. Singapore General Hospital: tel: 222 3322.

Security
Singapore is a safe city, even for women travelling alone. Attacks and muggings are rare, but it is still sensible to look after valuables in hotel rooms.

Diplomatic representation
UK: 30 Napier Road, tel: 473 9333. Open 8.30am–1pm and 2–5pm Monday to Friday.
US: 30 Hill Street, tel: 338 0251. Open 8.30am–5pm Monday to Friday.

Accommodation

Raffles Hotel

Hotel prices in Singapore are generally very reasonable despite the high occupancy rates. Expect to pay S$140–250 for a comfortable double room in a centrally-located hotel. The standard of accommodation in the large hotels is so high that they do not offer deluxe rooms. It is advisable to book a room in advance.

Airline companies such as Singapore Airlines and Qantas offer very competitive stopover deals. Usually included are the transfers to and from the airport and also a sightseeing tour of the city (from US$40 in a good hotel). To book a room on the spot may well cost 50 percent more. In addition, a surcharge of 14 percent is added to the in-house tariff.

The Singapore tourist office issues a brochure containing a list of the budget hotels in the city centre. If the cost of the room is less than S$80, then it is a good idea to inspect the room before making a firm reservation. In Singapore, air-conditioning is usually the norm. Camping is possible on the island of Sentosa and hire-tents are available. The island also boasts two well-equipped youth hostels. For more information, contact Sentosa Information Office, World Trade Centre, tel: 270 7888.

The 'boutique' hotels, as they are known, are predominantly small- to medium-sized houses, often old colonial-style buildings in fairly peaceful locations.

The most popular hotels are undoubtedly the ones near Orchard Road (the main shopping street), in the city centre (Marina Square) or in Chinatown.

Marina Mandarin: the atrium

Hotel selection

The following are hotel suggestions for various quarters of the city. They are listed according to three categories: $$$ = expensive; $$ = moderate; $ = inexpensive.

93

View from the Westin Stamford

Singapore Marriot Hotel

Orchard Road district

$$$Four Seasons Hotel, 190 Orchard Boulevard, tel: 734 1110, fax: 235 5131. Design a strong feature. Good fitness centre. **$$$Goodwood Park Hotel**, 22 Scotts Road, tel: 737 7411, fax: 732 8558. One of the few hotels with charm and a sense of history. **$$$Hyatt Regency**, 10 Scotts Road, tel: 738 1234. The Regency Club is a favourite with business people. **$$–$$$Mandarin Singapore**, 333 Orchard Road, tel: 737 4411, fax: 732 2361. Over a thousand rooms; in the middle of Orchard Road. **$$–$$$The Regent Singapore**, 1 Cuscaden Road, tel: 733 8888, fax: 732 8838. Stylish with excellent service. **$$–$$$Singapore Marriot Hotel**, 320 Orchard Road, tel: 535 5800, fax; 735 9800. After extensive renovations, the only concession to the hotel's Chinese past is its pagoda roof. **$Hotel Premier**, 22 Nassim Hill (near Tanglin Centre), tel: 733 9811, fax: 733 5595. Central but very quiet. Run by the hotel training association, so service varies.

City Centre (Marina Square)

$$$Raffles Hotel, 1 Beach Road, tel: 337 1886, fax: 339 7650. A residence rather than a hotel. The most expensive suites are furnished with carefully-selected antiques (from S$700). **$$$Marina Mandarin**, 6 Raffles Boulevard, Marina Square, tel: 338 3388, fax: 339 4977. The 70-m (220-ft) high atrium is the biggest in Southeast Asia. Try a cocktail here in the evening. Part of a busy shopping complex and linked by a corridor with the **$$$Pan Pacific Hotel Singapore**, 7 Raffles Boulevard, Marina Square, tel: 336 8111, fax: 339 1861. The glass lift gives a good view over the city centre and the Suntec City congress hall. **$$–$$$The Westin Stamford**, 2 Stamford Road, tel: 338 8585, fax: 337 1554. Within the luxurious Raffles City shopping centre. The tallest hotel in the world (226m/

741ft) and the best view of Singapore's skyline. A room with a view must be booked in advance. **$$Hotel New Otani**, 177A River Valley Road, tel: 338 3333, fax: 339 2854. Close to the Clarke Quay entertainment district. View over the Singapore River. **$–$$Allson Hotel Singapore**, 101 Victoria Street, tel: 336 0811, fax: 339 7019. Popular stopover hotel in a central location.

Chinatown
$$–$$$Duxton Hotel, 83 Duxton Road, tel: 227 7678, fax: 227 1232. 49 rooms. Meeting room and fitness room. Business equipment available. In the heart of the Tanjong Pagar conservation area. **$$Inn of the Sixth Happiness**, 9/37 Erskine Road, tel: 223 3266, fax: 223 7951. Old Chinese inn with 48 rooms. Furnished with antique Chinese furniture. **$–$$Apollo Hotel Singapore**, 405 Havelock Road, tel: 733 2081, fax: 733 1588. A well stocked Japanese department store, a good Japanese restaurant and a disco are part of the hotel. **$Damenlou**, 12 Ann Siang Road, tel: 221 1900, fax: 225 8500. Small, friendly hotel in the heart of Chinatown.

The Duxton

East Coast
$NTUC Pasir Ris Resort, 1 Pasir Ris Close, tel: 582 3322, fax: 582 9535. Hotel and holiday complex for Singaporeans. The 396 chalets are basic, but quite well equipped (no air-conditioning). Quiet countryside location by the water's edge.

Sentosa Island
$$$The Beaufort Singapore, Bukit Manis Road, Sentosa, tel: 275 0331, fax: 275 0228. Upmarket resort hotel with a stunning pool. **$$$Shangri-La Rasa Sentosa**, 101 Siloso Road, Sentosa, tel: 275 0100, fax: 275 0355. A restful tropical ambience and a huge swimming pool.

Shangri-La Rasa Sentosa

Budget hotels
Cost approximately S$85–120 per double room.

Sloane Court Hotel, 17 Balmoral Road, tel: 235 3311, fax: 733 9041. Tudor-style hotel with a popular restaurant and clean rooms (10-minute walk to the Newton MRT station; good bus connections). **VIP Hotel**, Balmoral Crescent, tel: 235 4277, fax: 235 2824. Swimming pool and large rooms in a smart residential estate (about 1km/1/2 mile from the Newton Circus). **YMCA International House**, 1 Orchard Road, tel: 336 6000, fax: 337 3140. Central location between Orchard Road and the city centre. Everybody welcome. **Metropole Hotel**, 41 Seah Street, tel: 336 3611, fax: 339 3610. Fifty-four rooms. Good, reasonably-priced rooms opposite Raffles.

Index

Accommodation......**93–5**
Alkaff Mansion **55**
Amoy Street **35**
Ann Siang Hill **33**
Ann Siang Road **35**
Arab Street **42–3**
Armenian Church of
St Gregory **24**
Art Museum **25**

Baghdad Street............**43**
Batam Island **61**
Boat Quay **22**
Botanical Gardens **56**
Buffalo Road **39–40**
Bukit Timah Nature
Reserve **57**
Bussorah Mall **43**
Butterfly Park and
Insect Kingdom **46**

Cable Car Plaza...........**46**
Cathedral of the Good
Shephard **25**
Cavenagh Bridge.........**21**
Cenotaph **26**
Central Beach...............**47**
Centre Point **28**
Changi **59**
Chettiar's Hindu
Temple.......................**55**
Chinaman Scholar
Gallery **37**
Chinatown **32–7**
Chinatown
Complex **36–7**
Chinatown Point..........**37**
Chinese Garden **48**
Chinese temples **65**
Christian Cemetery **24**
Cinemania **45**
City Hall......................**23**
climate..........................**6**
Club Street **33–4**
cottage industries **15**
Cuppage Terrace **28**
cuisines....................**71–6**
customs **63–5**

Desaru **60**
Duxton Hill **35–6**

East Coast Park **52**
economy **14–15**
Emerald Hill Road **29**
Empress Place
Building....................**21**
Esplanade Park............**26**
Eu Yan Sang
(chemist's)................**33**

Fantasy Island **45**
Far East Plaza, The...**30–1**
Feng Shui **66**
festivals **67–9**
flora and fauna **6–7**
Fort Canning Park **24**
Fort Siloso...................**47**
Forum Shopping Mall .**31**
Fountain Gardens **45–6**

General Post Office **21**
Geylang Serai Market .**51**
Goodwood Park
Hotel........................**30**

Haw Par Villa **56**
hawker stalls................**78**
Heeren, The..................**29**
history **16–17**

Indian temples.............**64**
Inn of Sixth
Happiness **35**

Jamae Mosque **37**
Japanese Garden..........**48**
Jim Thompson's...........**31**
Johor Bahru **60**
Joo Chiat Road **51–2**
Jurong......................**48–9**
Jurong Bird Park **49**
Jurong Crocodile
Paradise **49**

Katong district **52**
Keramat Iskandar
Shah **24–5**
Koon Seng Road **52**
Kukup...........................**60**
Kusu Island **53**

Lane Crawford
building.....................**30**
Lazarus Island **53**
Lee Ah Leng
Trading Company.....**41**
Leong San See
Temple.......................**41**
Liat Towers **30**
literature......................**66**
Little India.............**38–41**

Malacca **61**
Malay Village...............**50**
Mandai Orchid
Gardens.....................**58**
Marina Square **26**
Merlion...................**23, 46**
Ming Village **49**
Murray Terrace **35**

Nagore Durgha
Shrine.......................**34**
National Museum
and Art Gallery.........**25**
National Museum
Shop..........................**25**
Ngee Ann City **30**
Night Safari Park.........**57**
nightlife **82–3**

Orchard Emerald
Shopping Centre.......**29**
Orchard Plaza..............**28**
Orchard Point **28**
Orchard Road **27–31**
Orchard Towers **31**
Orchid Fantasy **45**
OUB Centre **20**
OUB Plaza **20–1**

Pacific Plaza **30**
Padang.........................**23**
Paragon Shopping
Centre **29**
Parliament House **22**
Pasir Ris Park **59**
Peninsula Plaza **23**
Peninsula Shopping
Centre **23–4**
people **8–11**
People's Park
Complex **37**
Peranakan Place **28–9**
Petain Road **41**
Pioneers of Singapore/
Surrender Chambers.**46**
Plaza Singapura...........**27**
politics **12–13**
Promenade Shopping
Centre **29**
Pulau Hantu **54**
Pulau Seking **54**
Pulau Ubin **54**

Raffles City................**26**
Raffles Hotel **26, 77**
Raffles Landing Site ...**22**
Raffles Place **20**
Raffles statues **22**
religions **11–12**
restaurants **71–8**

Satay Club..................**26**
Seng Poh Coffee Shop **58**
Sentosa **44–7**
Sentosa Food Centre ...**44**
Serangoon Road **39, 40**
shopping **27–31, 79–81**
Singapore Cricket
Club **23**

Singapore Harbour ..**58–9**
Singapore Performing
Arts Centre **26**
Singapore Post
Philatelic Bureau **28**
Singapore Recreation
Club **23**
Singapore River **22–3**
Singapore Science
Centre **49**
Singapore Sling **77**
Siong Lim Temple **59**
Specialist's Shopping
Centre **29**
Spice Garden **24**
Sri Mariamman
Temple.......................**32**
Sri Seng Aga Vinayagar
Temple.......................**52**
Sri Srinivasa Perumal
Temple.......................**41**
Sri Veeramakaliamman
Temple...................**40–1**
Sultan Mosque **43**
Sultan's Palace **43**
Supreme Court **23**
St Andrew's
Cathedral **23**

Tanglin Shopping
Centre **31**
Tang Dynasty
Village **48–9**
Tanjong Pagar
Heritage **36**
tea drinking **36**
Temple of
1,000 Lights.............**41**
Thian Hock Keng
Temple...................**34–5**
Time capsule **21**
tourist information **90**
transportation **85–8**

Underwater World **47**

Veeraswamy Road......**41**
Victoria Concert Hall
and Theatre **22**
Volcano Land...............**46**

Wak Hai Cheng Bio
Temple.......................**34**
Westin Stamford
Hotel **26**
Wisma Atria **30**
World Trade Centre **44**

Zhujiao Centre............**39**
Zoological Garden.......**57**